on track ...
Rancid

every album, every song

Paul Matts

sonicbondpublishing.com

Sonicbond Publishing Limited
www.sonicbondpublishing.co.uk
Email: info@sonicbondpublishing.co.uk

First Published in the United Kingdom 2022
First Published in the United States 2022

British Library Cataloguing in Publication Data:
A Catalogue record for this book is available from the British Library

Copyright Paul Matts 2022

ISBN 978-1-78952-187-0

Typeset in ITC Garamond & ITC Avant Garde
Printed and bound in England

Graphic design and typesetting: Full Moon Media

on track ...
Rancid

every album, every song

Paul Matts

sonicbondpublishing.com

Acknowledgements

Firstly I would like to thank Tim Armstrong, Matt Freeman, Brett Reed, Lars Frederiksen and Branden Steineckert. Plus Brett Gurewitz. And all others that helped Rancid in their inception, development and evolution as a punk rock band. Even when the music changed a little, the punk ethic remained. This I found so inspiring, and a rock in a society that lets you down continually.

Going further back, I would like to thank those bands that made Tim and co get up and play in the first place, particularly The Clash, whose music took me across the world.

I would also like to thank those young punks in the East Midlands, England, who turned me onto Rancid in the first place. So Dave, Mike, Dave again, Steve and countless others who I ran into in the 1990s. I had about given up on finding a new band who could get my blood pumping.

And finally, I would like to thank my family, in particular my wife Georgie, daughter Hannah and son Luke. Your love and support while I shut myself in the backroom writing this book meant more than you can ever imagine.

on track ...

Rancid

Contents

Foreword

So, here's the thing. Rancid are a punk rock band. But they're also so much more than that. Their shows will have punks, skins, hardcore crews, gangs, hooligans, straights and kids who are just getting into punk and whose mums and dads have dropped them off for the show. It's all-inclusive, everyone's welcome and they'll get an amazing punk rock show.

Daryl Smith – the guitarist with UK street-punk heroes Cock Sparrer – wrote those words in 2015.

My favourite music has always been the stuff that raised my blood temperature, stuff that made the hairs on the back of my neck stand up, and, crucially, stuff that's inclusive. Music should help unite the world. As a kid, I loved noise – big guitars; a wall of sound; a big, brash chorus that didn't piss about. I didn't pay attention to the lyrics back then, *see*. The Sex Pistols thrilled the life out of me. They were so exciting and made me want to jump right out of my skin. It took me away from my everyday life. I became more lyrically aware as I got older. Joe Strummer then gave me an education as The Clash became the only band that mattered. It's about unity, *see*.

I experienced some of the impact of the first punk wave as a kid: if only by realising the hatred my parents and their kind had for it. Unifying the world? Not much chance in the late-1970s with that lot. Their apathy made it more appealing, of course, and made me feel slightly marginalised. I needed a place to go. I needed to feel part of something. Plenty of decent bands came along as the years passed and I grew older, but none had the impact of The Clash and the Pistols on me. I had given up on getting that thrill I used to get: when music spoke directly and made me feel unstoppable.

But then I heard lyrics written from the heart and performed from the gut. I wasn't really prepared for the impact Tim Armstrong, Lars Frederiksen, Matt Freeman and Brett Reed were to have on my life in the 1990s. Their music may not have sounded as if it was coming from another planet, as it did back in the 1970s, but Rancid got my fists clenched and made my attitude positive. I felt like I could conquer the world. *Let's Go* was the album in question; 'Radio', the track. It was written for the likes of me. That was how I interpreted it anyway – a story of my own musical upbringing; it didn't piss about. The chorus words spoke so directly: 'When I got the music, I got a place to go'.

My aim in writing this book is to provide a guide to Rancid's officially released music. Working chronologically, it will treat every album as a destination on a journey and will provide my interpretation of the band's musical and lyrical evolution. It will link the band to the punk network they've always championed so earnestly. Rancid have released nine studio albums, all to a consistently high standard. There are no duff records in their catalogue. In addition to the complete studio albums, there are singles, EPs, split releases and compilations. Each official studio album will get its own section, including any expanded editions with bonus tracks. Singles released from an album are covered in the same section – this applies to promotional singles, which are particularly relevant in the United States, as the *Billboard* chart is determined by radio airplay rather than actual physical sales as in the UK. Stand-alone singles are also covered, as are the splits, compilations and rarities. Finally, there's a section on some unofficial releases/bootlegs.

Maybe the effect will be the same as on me in the 1990s, reigniting a flame I assumed had died out. Enjoy!

Introduction and Background

Two matters need to be made clear from the outset. Firstly, it's important to
understand the state of music – and specifically punk rock – in the late-1980s.
Secondly, it's crucial to appreciate the relationship between childhood friends
and Rancid founder members Matt Freeman and Tim Armstrong.

In the late-1980s, mainstream popular-music artists had gotten lazy, self-
righteous and insincere. The well-meant message of *Live Aid* – with humanity
at its core – had given way to formulaic smugness. The sounds of superstars
such as Michael Jackson, George Michael and any number of girl and boy
bands, were complacent; banal, at best. The same applied to the *MTV*-friendly
hair metal that vomited itself out of every doorway. How had it come to *this?*
Art – especially cutting-edge youth culture – thrives on disaffection. After
decades of unease, the Cold War was thawing. Relations between east and
west improved, with Ronald Reagan and Mikhail Gorbachev working closer
than had previously seen between US and Soviet leaders. The Berlin Wall
came down: Germany was reunified. Things were getting better on the face of
it. Populations saw prosperity for those lucky enough to *succeed*. Greed was
good, or so the slogan said – not necessarily the fuel for a healthy, thrusting
music scene though.

Record companies held the power in the music industry, as they had for
many years of course. In the 1980s, greed and wealth mattered, and record
companies were unwilling to take risks. If an artist didn't promise big bucks
in return for investment, it wasn't gonna happen. Music imitated life, and
record companies went where the money lay. For those on the wrong end of
capitalism, life is always tough. For every wolf on Wall Street, there were several
mutts on shit street: all scratching around in the gutters for the scraps.

Thankfully, the underground music scene had a small, sympathetic, healthy
pulse that slowly began to throb with an increasing resonance. It attracted
those mutts from shit street. The birth of the indie scene halfway through the
decade was significant. It took the do-it-yourself punk ethos championed by the
likes of Crass to a new level. Rough Trade and Factory Records in the UK were
true independent operations, as was Sub Pop in the US. The focus was the
other side of life in the 1980s – songs about isolation, solitude and suffering:
the unspoken, uncomfortable, poverty-stricken edgy bit.

In the first half of the 1980s, punk continued its evolution. Several subgenres
emerged, each providing their own flag wavers. So, the work of the Sex Pistols,
Ramones, The Clash and others was continued by US hardcore pioneers
Black Flag, Minor Threat and Dead Kennedys, horror-punk heroes Misfits
and Canada's D.O.A. GBH and Discharge led the UK hardcore scene, with
street acts like Cock Sparrer giving their own street interpretation of punk.
Tim Armstrong took note. New York had continually grabbed the plaudits
and the attention with a succession of bands, and legendary venues such as
CBGB. In California, another scene had emerged: more political than its NYC
counterpart. Bands such as Dead Kennedys courted controversy with just their

11

name when they started in 1978. Their direct hardcore style inspired another generation. However, as the decade went on, many of these seminal bands, split. Any scene would miss inspirational giants like Black Flag, Minor Threat, Misfits, The Clash and Cock Sparrer. All these bands – incredibly – had called it a day by 1986. With the Pistols long-since imploded and The Damned going goth, the punk scene was soon on its heels. The punk cause seemed in retreat. Sex Pistol and Los Angeles' number-one punk disc jockey Steve Jones summed it up as only he can in his 2-16 autobiography *Lonely Boy: Tales From A Sex Pistol:* 'There was a weird period – the mid-1980s – when no one seemed to give a fuck about punk. Now it's gone back to being a big deal again, and it feels like it won't ever go away. But then it just seemed like something that had happened but was now over'.

By the mid-1980s, the first wave of American hardcore had also developed problems. The 2017 movie *Turn It Around: The Story of East Bay Punk,* stated, 'The once-vibrant local scene became overwrought with violence, corruption and racism'. Things had become dark, metallic, gloomy and restrictive; not to mention uniform. Since when had punk rock ever been about uniformity: literal or metaphorical?

Punk still attracted the misfits, but the arrival of indie music meant punk had a rival for their attention. This gave punk yet another problem – as well as a sudden lack of top-level bands and divisive scenes, its rebel public had more musical choice. It could go for Bad Religion on one hand, or The Smiths on the other. Original punk kids moved into new scenes, often never to return. Punk had to fight its corner.

In the late-1980s, a community over the San Francisco bridge on the East Bay, came together. Its goal was to bring unity and enjoyment back into punk. A volunteer collective centred around 924 Gilman Street, Berkeley, began putting on shows in late-1986 and provided the support network any true scene *needs*. Diversity in ethnicity, musical style, image and performance, were encouraged. It reinvigorated the very punk ideal: anyone could do it and could play what they wanted. Little did those involved know the impact this would go on to have on punk rock worldwide. It's fair to say that what followed five years later was nothing short of punk's second coming. The 1991 punk breakout owed 924 Gilman Street *so* much. Tim Armstrong helped explain why to *Hitlist* magazine in October 2001: 'It was so open-minded, and a great climate to be creative and do some cool shit. Gilman was a climate you could play punk rock and ska and not get moshed on. That's something you gotta think about'.

Tim Armstrong and Matt Freeman first met as young kids in Albany, California. They remained school acquaintances rather than outright friends until they were in the same music class, where they had a crack at 'Blue Suede Shoes' to win a prize in a music contest. They didn't succeed, but more importantly, their partnership began. Picking up punk influences ranging from The Clash to Circle Jerks, they formed a band called – appropriately – The Noise: which mutated into Basic Radio. Tim and Matt were at 924 Gilman

Street from the first show on 31 December 1986. In an example of the Gilman camaraderie, Matt – in time – took the weekend's debris to the local dump, in return for free admission to shows.

Operation Ivy came together in 1987 and featured vocalist Jesse Michaels (Shrik), drummer Dave Mello (Animal), guitarist Tim Armstrong (Lint) and bassist Matt Freeman (McCall). They personified the Gilman punk ideal – Liberty: the freedom to do what you want and break conventions. Talk about being *influential*. And talk about being *creative*. Operation Ivy took the joy and energy of 2 Tone and ska music – with its offbeat emphasis – added the ferocity of Bay Area hardcore, and presto! – ska punk was born: a union of The Specials, hardcore and melody. Jesse Michaels described the band's arrival in an interview with *Alternative Music Press* in 2017:

It's kind of a fun challenge to go into a room full of grumpy hardcore people and try to win them over. At that time (the late-1980s), the first wave of hardcore was really sort of tired – a lot of the best bands had broken up, and there were a lot of bands that were doing something a little bit more energetic. It was fun to do something new in that context when everything felt a little burned out.

With Michaels' politically charged vocals, the band were heroes of Gilman Street, and developed a cult following. Also, they were Gilman Street's go-to band – if a show needed playing, even at short notice, they'd do it. Matt Freeman told *Hitlist* magazine, 'It was like, we'll be here because we'll be here anyway. We just have to remember to bring our equipment this time'.

Later in 1987, *Maximumrocknroll* magazine released two compilation albums, both titled *Turn It Around*. Operation Ivy's 'I Got No' and 'Officer' were included. This now-highly-collectable record was the first time Matt and Tim appeared on any release anywhere. The six-track EP *Hectic* was recorded soon after and released on Lookout! Records. 1000 copies were pressed and sold out: unheard of for a grassroots band in 1987. Larry Livermore set up *Lookout!* Records in 1987. *Hectic* reeks of do-it-yourself: black-and-white cover; information sheet inside.

A United States tour followed; the band and a couple of friends travelling in a 1969 Chrysler Newport, feeding themselves cheese sandwiches out of the vehicle's boot. Operation Ivy's popularity grew and grew. They had invented something fresh, something new, and major record labels – not for the only time in Tim and Matt's live's – began to take notice.

Work began on the band's only full album, with a stop/start series of recording sessions with Gilman sound engineer Radley Hirsch. Eventually, the album was recorded in a week at San Francisco's Sound And Vision studio, and produced by Kevin Army. The result – *Energy* – is an essential slice of progressive punk rock, and was released in May 1989. It inspired a whole generation of ska punk acts like Sublime, King Prawn and Reel Big Fish. Many went on to cover Operation Ivy songs. *Energy* remains one of Lookout!'s biggest sellers. It's incredible. Songs like 'Sound System' and 'Unity' were exactly what the punk scene needed in 1989: fresh songs with a sonic that broke new ground. Rancid still play 'Knowledge' in their sets, and fellow Gilman pioneers Green Day also cover it: often picking out an audience member to join them.

But it was already the beginning of the end. Before the album release party at Gilman on 28 May, Operation Ivy imploded. Tim explained:

> We decided we didn't want to do it anymore. I remember me and Jesse, we were on Telegraph (Road, Berkeley), I was buying him some beer, and we went to Cloyne Court. There was an old volleyball court, and we sat there. Me and him talked about how the band wasn't really what it was when it started. It was like a mutual thing.

The band often experienced internal conflict, and this was initially channelled into making great music. But such volatile cocktails are not made to last. Popularity often breeds a new attitude. Things got serious: business-like even. Matt told *Hitlist* in 2012: 'It was almost like people started taking it more seriously than they should have'. Op Ivy have remained tight-lipped about the split: no one blames anyone else. *It wasn't the same anymore* seems an appropriate paraphrase.

However, there was a darker side brewing. The effect the band breakup had on Tim Armstrong was almost catastrophic. He was already a drinker – like his father – and this had already begun to affect Operation Ivy. Tim told *Hitlist*: 'One time he (Radley) came to pick me up, and I was too fucking drunk to record'.

With Op Ivy's demise, Tim's drinking escalated. With Matt by his side, several new bands ensued. Generator were a metal-punk band; Shaken 69 were ska. Downfall were the pick of this bunch, featuring Dave Mello once more on drums. They played some rapturously-received gigs, and recorded a couple of songs which appeared on compilation albums. But they soon fell apart, Tim remembering, 'Just how Op Ivy didn't feel right at the end, Downfall didn't feel right either'. Matt provided more support and encouragement to his friend but eventually had to get on with his own life. He joined MDC and went out on tour, with Tim as his roadie. Matt – with a growing reputation as a bassist – then joined The Gr'ups.

Meanwhile, Tim was heading for oblivion, and fast. He was hospitalised three times between 1989 and 1990 due to alcohol and drug misuse. His mother eventually refused to let him stay with her. The nadir arrived when Tim was forced to seek refuge at a Salvation Army shelter. He worked in return for a bed for the night. Candid as ever, he described the situation as, 'a humiliating place, but I had nowhere else to go'. But when you're at the bottom, you have two choices – you give up, or you fight and go the other way: up. It was at this point that Tim found inner strength: the kind required to not drink anymore.

Matt was pleased to hear this, but was busy with The Gr'ups, who took up much of his time. So, Tim had to prove himself to his friend. Months passed. Tim remained dry. But Matt was always ready for the phone call that told him his friend had fallen off again. It didn't come. And after a while, the pair started jamming. When you've got the music, you've got a place to go. Tim recounted the period fondly: 'Matt was in The Gr'ups. It didn't matter. It was like all I wanted, to be sober and hang out with my best friend again'.

With royalty payments from *Energy* finally filtering through, Tim could afford his $100-a-month rent. That meant a lot. He was making things work, paying his way. And he could concentrate on writing music: hardcore punk rock music. He had anger to get out, *see*. And after about a year, Matt had faith in Tim once more. Matt left The Gr'ups to concentrate on making music with his friend. He reminisced in 2012: 'After that year was up, I cut The Gr'ups off faster than. I never looked back. It was like, bye bye'.

Meanwhile, out in the punk rock landscape, things were changing fast. More and more bands wanted to be part of the East Bay scene. Outsiders came in, fans grew in number. And record company sharks circulated. By the end of the decade, local bands were signing to majors: starting with Sweet Baby. Sweet Baby shared a space alongside Op Ivy on those *Turn It Around* compilations. It was the beginning of the end of the original tight-knit Gilman scene.

Further afield, alternative music was infiltrating the mainstream. Bands like Nirvana, Dinosaur Jr. and Mudhoney – grunge bands with clear punk influences – were making waves in Seattle and across the country. Nirvana's debut *Bleach* was released on Sub Pop in 1989. Come 1991, this new alternative had passed being merely infiltrating: it took over. The days of complacent half-assed superstars having it all their own way, were over. Nirvana's second album *Nevermind* saw to that.

East Bay heroes Sweet Children – now Green Day – had released two albums on *Lookout!* by the end of 1991. The second of these was *Kerplunk*, which remains the label's best seller. Green Day were on their way to becoming the biggest punk band around. Their third record *Dookie* (1994) was to become punk's highest-selling album of all time. It was released on *Reprise*: a major-distributed label. Green Day's Billie Joe Armstrong and Mike Dirnt were from the same Gilman Street scene as Tim and Matt. The Offspring – another Californian pop-punk outfit – were also on their way to becoming huge.

Tim and Matt could've been forgiven in 1991 for thinking they'd missed the boat. The pair recruited Brett Reed on drums. Brett – a skater punk kid – could hardly play, mind. So, obviously, Rancid's initial progress was not as seamless as it would've been had Tim and Matt opted for a seasoned drummer. But by going with a novice who was joining his first band, Rancid created a brotherhood. Brett was a street kid who liked it fast – just as well, given the music the trio were creating: frenetic, angry songs performed from the gut, warts and all. He'd only been playing on a cheap drum kit, for two months. His challenge was clear: he had to get his shit together. Luckily, Tim and Matt were prepared to give Brett time and guidance. Brett told *In Music We Trust* in 1998: 'I totally sucked! But those guys stuck with me and taught me'.

Matt Freeman, on the other hand, could play so well and fast that it appeared he must have at least six or seven fingers on his left hand. He was now a top bass player: not common in punk rock. The role was often handed to someone on the basis the instrument had two fewer strings than a guitar. Therefore, Matt not only had to be patient with his friend Tim whilst he proved himself but also with a new rhythm-section partner. It shows one hell of a lot about Matt as a character.

The trio started jamming in 1990, playing at private parties and around Gilman. Tim wrote lyrics and the band practised at Gilman on a Sunday afternoon: in return for cleaning the venue's toilets. Matt grimaced as he recalled the horror of those days to *Hitlist*: 'I thought garbage man was hard. Those toilets were the most disgusting thing ever'. It was a grassroots start – like any band – but character-building. There was no special treatment given just because half of Operation Ivy were in this new band called Rancid.

Rancid (EP) (1992)

Personnel:
Tim 'Lint' Armstrong: vocals, guitar
Matt 'McCall' Freeman: vocals, bass
Brett Reed: drums
Producer: Andy Ernst
Label: Lookout!
Release dates: US: 2 September 1992, UK: N/A
Running time: 11:05

Some original fans gave the band's debut EP the title *The Bottle,* due to its cover artwork. Some also call it the *I'm Not the Only One* EP, after the lead track. However, it was officially released as simply *Rancid*, consisting of five songs with lyrics reflecting the lives of the people who wrote them: street-level urban punk rock songs.

Tim's raging guitar performance on the EP isn't surprising. His battle with drink and drugs has been mentioned, and the anger and frustration pent up inside him, very definitely – to my ears – comes over in his six-string work. It's feisty and sprays across the five tracks like an out-of-control aerosol can. Brett Reed's drumming is, frankly, miraculous, considering how long he'd been playing. But the standout feature is without doubt Matt Freeman's bass-playing. His speed and dexterity are astonishing. Lead vocals are split between Matt and Tim. Matt's rich and full growl has a highly distinctive quality. Tim's slurred, gritty and soulful delivery is often hard to decipher. Given their quite-different sounds, the two also combine and interchange to great effect: a definite Rancid characteristic, moving forward.

By the end of summer 1992, the three had recorded ten of their best tracks at Art of Ears in Hayward, San Francisco: a studio where many punk bands had gone before and would after. Production was by studio engineer Andy Ernst. Five of the recordings ended up on *Rancid.* The sound is very raw, but no other sonic would've been appropriate at this early juncture. Punk is raw, and *Rancid* is at odds with the more-melodic offerings of The Offspring and Green Day in the early-1990s.

Lyrically, Rancid focused on street themes; on darker struggles. The abused, the homeless, the have-nots; greed vs hunger; Tim's own anger and humility. However, Lookout! founder and owner Larry Livermore was not a fan. Brett Reed explained why to *In Music We Trust*: 'Larry Livermore didn't like Rancid. He put out that first seven-inch, we always thought, as a favour to Tim and Matt since Operation Ivy did so well'.

The EP was only released as a 7". Test pressings were made on blue translucent vinyl in a plain white sleeve. Copies issued on red vinyl (nice) have also been reported: worth a few quid each, I'd say. The full pressings were made on black vinyl. The sleeve is very much that of a street-punk single: black and white, with a bottle featured in the front cover artwork. Earlier copies folded out to a four-page booklet, with song lyrics and back-cover artwork featuring an incendiary device: a street bomb, packed with sticks of dynamite. Later pressings had a glossy two-page booklet. It's the kind of record we've all bought at a show, to support the band, to support the scene. These are the most important purchases.

Side One

'I'm Not the Only One' (Music: Rancid, Lyrics: Armstrong)

This gives an early taste of classic Rancid ingredients. Matt's verse-vocal delivery is rapid, followed sharply by a chorus in terrace style. Tim joins him: together they burst their lungs. Rancid have always, *always*, had killer choruses: an essential characteristic of street punk. Us fans like to clench our fists and shout along, *see*. Audiences at Rancid shows have been among the loudest sing-along sessions I've ever been to.

The introduction is at half-speed; the E and Bb guitar chords just about containing the venom. It then explodes with natural high-octane ferocity, Tim's guitar now utilising A and F shapes, spraying angry noise. Matt's lightning-quick bass line is immediately prominent: the hammering multi-note runs being the band's trump card at this point in their career. Brett's drumming has a swing to it, like he's playing along with the music rather than putting down a timing frame for the others to follow.

Tim's lyrics are defiant – seeing through family abuse and supporting the girl on the receiving end. Life on the street sure is better than her life behind closed doors.

> She could no longer live with the lying
> Her family tried to control her feelings
> It just gave her life a deeper meaning

The words are relatable to anyone who has had the misfortune of suffering abuse: domestic or otherwise. Choose the alternative and get out if you can. Be brave. Many will support you, as they've been through it too.

'Battering Ram' (Music: Rancid, Lyrics: Armstrong)

It's Tim's turn to deliver the rapid-fire verse. His vocal is soulful: spat, shouted and gargled. The number's high-speed aggression matches the message. The lyric is, again, defiant: extremely. No matter what the problem, be strong and you can get through. The problem may be addiction, abuse, money or dealers. Or maybe it's all of these and more. This may mean moving on, leaving people behind. Matt takes the knockout line as the music stops dead: 'Been running my whole life, and I'm still running'.

The verse chord structure – F/C# – gives the track its hardcore character – not technically difficult, but effective with Matt working flat-out beneath. The song was a live favourite in those early Gilman days and has been a regular feature on setlists over time.

Side Two
'The Sentence' (Music: Rancid, Lyrics: Armstrong)
One minute and 37 seconds of blistering punk rock. It has a smash-'n'-grab feel, with superb vocal interchange throughout between Tim and Matt, great siren-style guitar, and busy electrifying bass.

Picking up from 'Battering Ram', we get an insight into Lint's (Tim) mind at the time. It's a positive, focused response to the issues that plagued him pre-1991. It's very philosophical, alluding to awareness of the sentence imposed on those who realise the corruption surrounding them. It's very positive and implies nothing is wasted: even the effect of corruption.

> My life's a blessing
> Understand my aggression
> I don't regret nothing
> It's all been a lesson

Aggression can be channelled. This lyric points to the future, tugging at my heartstrings in the process. Music makes life better. It gives us some place to go. You see, Rancid spoke to people like me.

> Sometimes I'm a total wreck
> I want to break someone's neck
> I get a subwoofer going
> Four 12s get my bloodstream flowing

'The Sentence' is almost a prequel to 'Radio' from the band's second album *Let's Go*: the song that reminded me of the power of music. It's also the first example of lyrics Rancid would paraphrase in later material (In this case, again 'Radio'): 'Me and my friend, we got the music/Like a loaded gun, we're gonna use it'.

'Media Controller' (Music: Rancid, Lyrics: Armstrong)
The riffy intro opens a track loaded with terrific punk guitar work – an innovative riff, with fluent, attacking Chuck Berry-style rock-'n'-roll solos over D and A chords. Matt's vocal has savage attack and allows room for Tim to finish off the verses. The huge chorus is another early example of that Rancid trademark.

It's a sinister, dark street story of street violence at a show. Scumbags are sent into a gig by corrupt officials working with a fucked-up promoter. The inevitable result is a shooting, with bullets from a Glock pistol aimed at fans. The band are pressured into co-operating with the corrupt officials but refuse to do so. But it's time the story was told. Storytelling was to become another regular ingredient of the band's songs.

> The kid unloaded his Glock into the urban blight
> Bullets sprayed the car and we drove into the night

19

We lived to tell the story and I'm gonna tell you
The State of the Union and the State of California

The term 'urban blight' is another phrase recycled in future Rancid work.

'Idle Hands' (Music: Rancid, Lyrics: Armstrong)

This is the record's only track that includes an experimental element. The track is bookended with a spaced section created by clean, phased guitar, subtle percussion and bass. A high-tempo psychobilly rhythm provides the backing. Tim's vocal is comparatively restrained; his gravel tone displaying soul – again, another characteristic appearing time-and-again on future recordings, but easy to overlook amidst the ferocity.

The song's theme is the despair of being homeless, isolation, and slipping back into the world of addiction and frustration – a very hard, candid set of words, but with a positive outlook and a welcome dash of humour.

Spent some time in a shelter down in Webster
You think I'm going back, you must be joking
If I ever forget how bad it was to be homeless
I must still be high from the dope I was smoking

Rancid (LP) (1993)

Personnel:
Tim Armstrong, Matt Freeman: vocals, guitar
Brett Reed: drums
Producer: Donnell Cameron
Recorded at Westbeach Recorders, Los Angeles
Label: Epitaph
Release date: 10 May 1993
Chart positions: Did not chart
Running time: 34:17

One of the most prudent moves Tim Armstrong made early on was to pass a demo of his new band to Brett Gurewitz. The Bad Religion guitarist had set up his Epitaph record label in the early-1980s and was impressed by the three-piece's sound and approach. Not only did Epitaph go on to release the band's material until 2000, but with Tim they later formed Hellcat Records, which subsequently released the rest of Rancid's official output. Hellcat has contributed massively to the punk network, with an increasing roster of exciting material by new acts and punk legends. The *Give 'Em The Boot* compilations introduced a whole generation of bands to new fans, and vice versa.

Rancid were becoming better and better, playing gritty punk rock. They were angry too – angry at the demise of Op Ivy; angry at the gradual breakup of the Gilman scene; angry at outsiders and users; angry at their own personal situations. Therefore, their sound had the speed of hardcore and is indeed classed as such by many. As Matt told *Slap* magazine in 2000, 'We were pissed'. The street punk influence was also clear, with shouty terrace choruses galore. Rancid were about unity, even at this early stage: something they maintained and encouraged throughout their career. This point is important.

Rancid is a punk rock album – nothing else; no experimental meanderings; no sign of Op Ivy ska punk, nor any pandering to the newly-converted punk masses by trying to write a *Billboard* hit single with heavy MTV rotation potential.

'Urban blight' is a term used on the band's debut EP, and is used once again here in the opening cut 'Adina'. The two words describe the album's theme: the city's dirt, splattered across a series of stories, characters and situations. It is a metaphor, obviously, for the human suffering, and being trapped in a city; true and believable because that was the life Tim – especially – had been living in Berkeley – drug addicts, alcoholism, homelessness, dirge, crime, rats, cockroaches. Inequality. The feeling you're being cheated. Exploitation. But at the same time, camaraderie.

Production was undertaken by Donnell Cameron at his Westbeach Recorders in Los Angeles. Donnell had worked with the likes of NOFX, and went on to work with Blink-182, Sublime, Voodoo Glowskulls and Avenged Sevenfold.

Rancid was issued in May 1993, on vinyl, cassette and compact disc. The artwork – courtesy of Tracy Cox – is a painting of a man aiming a pistol. The original Rancid logo is used: with the band's name seemingly stamped on the front cover. This logo was ditched for the next album and for most releases afterwards but did make a reappearance much later. Mackie McAleer produced the remaining artwork, consisting of song lyrics, and a series of Gilman gig posters featuring some familiar and unknown names. We punk fans all love a do-it-yourself gig poster. The photograph under the Gilman Street sign on the back cover – taken by Kathy Bauer – is of a punk (Tim), a skater (Brett) and a muso (Matt).

Rancid remains essential listening to this day, with punk rock purists maintaining it's the band's best. Many compare it to the classic fifth album (also called *Rancid*). It flashes by like a high-speed car chase through the dark-and-dingy metropolis in the early hours. It sounds dangerous. Matt's bass-playing is, again, astounding. Even non-musicians refer to its speed, dexterity and melody; it's pushed high in the mix, easy to highlight. Brett keeps up with Matt: no easy task. But like The Rolling Stones' Charlie Watts (RIP), Brett's playing works with everything going on around him. This gives the *swing* characteristic and helps bind things together.

'Adina' (Armstrong, Freeman)

The words 'Let's go!!' scream out as 'Adina' explodes from the speakers. The breakneck bass from Matt is phenomenal. Siren guitars, wail, interposed with six-string lead flurries. 'Hey! Hey!' is chanted over and over, and we're off. The first verse is taken by Matt: 'I want to go where the action is/I want to fly through the urban blight'.

Tim takes the chorus. They swap for the final verse and chorus, sung over C, F and G chords – a regular Rancid backing structure – Tim's slur working across Matt's growl. But lyrically, it isn't about the excitement of urban living, but its struggle. Urban blight is the background to a tale where the main character Adina is constantly down on her luck, nothing working out, moving on but not moving up.

> How did she know the roof would cave in again and again?
> Beat up, bruised, a record that's broken
> Adina's crying again

'Adina' sets the record's tone sonically and lyrically. It was a big number at early Rancid shows.

'Hyena' (Armstrong, Freeman)

Matt's rolling, jazzy bass line sets the track up with real swing, and stays in place when Tim's guitar chords and Brett's snappy rhythm come in. It's high-octane Bourbon Street bop punk. The intro is used again as a bridge, reintroducing this characteristic. The verses, however, are spitting punk rock, with Tim's vocal difficult to decipher; the third verse especially, with the distortion effect added to Tim's voice. The chorus is big, inviting crowds at shows to punch the air when shouting the title.

The lyric is the life of an outsider – one who is unaffected by politics or authority, fighting and scrapping for anything they can get; feeding off leftovers, scraps. Like a hyena. It even hints at Tim's mother turning him away at the height of his alcoholism, leading him to live this life: 'I'm a nomad to travel/ Concrete class stone and gravel'. It's about survival, doing what's necessary, scrounging, and opportunism where it's needed.

The track appeared on the very first *Punk-O-Rama* compilation, alongside the likes of The Offspring, NOFX and Bad Religion.

'Detroit' (Armstrong, Freeman)

A sign of the Rancid sound many were to embrace in future years. A huge chorus, but with a slight easing of the tempo. This could've been an MTV favourite had it been released later. The bass line is unbelievable. twiddling, popping, with more notes on it than there appear to be on the fretboard! Tim's guitar solo, holds its own with a gorgeous single-string run lifting the track off, followed by swift lead work.

It has a comparatively heartwarming storyline too: the comfort of time spent off the street, in the arms of a hooker, as the band hit Detroit, on tour: respite from the urban blight. Tim's vocal is slurred as ever, gravelly, but now with soul. The backing has more space in it, and the lyrics are thus easy to follow. The chorus is slowed down, delivered staccato over a D/A/G/D chord progression: great to sing over, with the words taken by Matt. The pair finish the chorus off in unison: 'Some run, some fight/I've got a good feeling in a bad city tonight'.

'Rats In the Hallway' (Armstrong, Freeman)

The frenetic pace returns on this early classic. It's played regularly in the band's sets, right to the present day. It's a firm favourite, listed in many Rancid fan's top song list.

Following the slight respite of 'Detroit', the lyric returns to familiar themes: squalor, disease and decay. The lyrics are some of the band's starkest: a story in the seedy streets of early-hours San Francisco. Not for the fainthearted – tales of shooting up, meeting up with other addicts with the mutual goal of getting high. A twelve-year-old boy gets shot: his reward for being out in the cold in these drug-laden streets. He had it coming, according to his landlord.

The sonic, matches. A hedonistic high-speed drive through these streets – never pausing, never slowing down. It's exhilarating, with classic early-Rancid punk rock ingredients. Tim's vocal is of someone knowing exactly his subject matter – he lays bare his soul with his gravelly, biting, desperate performance. Again, a distortion effect is used intermittently on his singing. Stunning.

'Another Night' (Armstrong, Freeman)

Against a lightning punk backing, a story is told of homelessness and drugs; the desperation of it all, juxtaposed against Oakland's beautiful nocturnal skyline. The song paints a picture of the struggle, despite these Californian skies. But there's a glimpse of positivity in the lyric: that there is a way out if you want it badly enough: 'All I wanna do is keep on trying'.

The chorus has a nice C to A-minor chord change, which lifts it before dropping back into F, G and C once more. A nice variation.

'Animosity' (Armstrong, Freeman)

A monster. Tim's deep guitar, distorts, as Matt's lightning bass, underpins. The chorus is arranged fantastically well, using staccato delivery once more. Hatred, unease and hostility, burn away in the lyric about street violence. The helicopter sound effect and siren-style guitar, add to the street-riot feel. It's a track that raises the blood temperature; a real exciting cut.

This is a standout. The slight pause at 90 seconds as Tim's guitar rings and Brett eases off the drums, is especially effective at creating a calm after the storm – as if the rioters have eased back; as if the cops think they've regained control: which they haven't. The full-on power returns, and the riot comes back full pelt. The music's ferocity is re-engaged, and some.

'Outta My Mind' (Armstrong, Freeman, Dinnwitty)

The album's sixth cut is slightly edgy, its atmosphere uneasy. It's co-written with Eric Dinnwitty of ska punk band The Uptones.

The bass line is much slower basic root note stuff, allowing room for Tim's vocal and guitar to take centre stage. The bass only gets fast and busy immediately before Tim's guitar break. 'Outta My Mind' shows the way for many slower future Rancid songs, allowing Tim to showcase his voice. Hell, the lyrics are even easy to make out. In a perfect marriage of sonic and theme, the song's uneasy backing is matched by the lack of trust between drug dealers and users, who live in a world needing each other but not trusting each other: 'Senses were corroded/You know that I was loaded/You were dealing, I was reeling'.

'Whirlwind' (Armstrong, Freeman)

The first of two absolute hurricane tracks, raising the velocity another notch. 'Whirlwind' was a big song in the band's early days: a setlist regular. The vocal arrangements on this and the next cut 'Rejected', are similar. Tim's word-packed verse gives way to Matt's sing-along chorus; his growl suiting both titles. As on the previous track, there's room in the verse for Tim to reach out as a vocalist, helped again by the largely root-note backing. Matt's bass is again restrained.

The lyric focusses on a city going to ruin, dragged down with the industry that used to be its lifeblood. The metaphors are superb: 'Every city got an artery where the blood breaks down'. The entire final verse is a reference to Tim's Dad, and signs off in tragic spirituality.

My old man worked his troubled life in a nowhere dead end
He drank the pain away
I'll be damned if that's me having my dreams robbed
The working class carries a country that has been rotting inside for years
The rigs cuffed my old man in the front yard
I saw through my eyes of tears
A promise to go to heaven won't put salvation in sight

In my view, these are some of Tim's best early lyrics – slightly autobiographical, loaded with stark references and ugly symbolism, but racked with social comment.

'Rejected' (Armstrong, Freeman)

The second of the back to back hurricane tracks. A nice interchange in the first two verses, gives way to a Matt Freeman monster one-word chorus. Matt then takes the final verse alone.

This is a highlight in any Rancid show. It allows fans who go way back, to show those who only came to hear 'Time Bomb' and 'Fall Back Down', where Rancid came from. Check Matt as he stretches those 'e's in the chorus over the E/C/G/A chord sequence: 'Re-e-e-e-e-jec-ted'. The subject matter – of being outcast for any reason (often due to being a punk) – is something many Rancid fans relate to. It can apply to the socio-economic class too – the working classes shoved to one side in favour of those who wear the right clothes, eat at the correct restaurants and have friends with benefits.

'Injury' (Armstrong, Freeman)

Ever felt let down by someone you put your faith in (or money), who then used you, stabbing you in the back in the process? Well, this song is for you. Again, the fight is on behalf of the working classes: continually exploited for the material and economic gain of the rich and privileged. It's a very angry lyric, delivered with a barrage of expletives which ram the rage to breaking point, hence the title. The rolling chord pattern and fists-aloft chorus, all contribute. The bridge consisting of a twist in the chord sequence is very effective.

'The Bottle' (Armstrong, Freeman)

This is the title some gave the band's debut EP issued on Lookout! a year earlier. A self-explanatory lyric written by Tim – someone who has experienced the desperation of alcoholism; the need to get drunk to block out real life, and the acknowledgment that drinking is the one thing the protagonist is good at. Also, the reality of turning to the booze when becoming depressed, which of course makes it all worse. Bleak.

Tim and Matt take vocal duties in roughly equal measure, with Matt's trebly bass, guiding this high-speed number. This is a technique the band used a lot in the early days: the bass taking the melody, the guitar used rhythmically.

'Trenches' (Armstrong, Freeman)

Ask Rancid fans for this album's standout cuts, and chances are a good percentage will list 'Trenches'. It's a good example of excellent sequencing: placing such a strong number deep in the LP's running order. It's one of the reasons albums are so important, as opposed to the downloading of isolated tracks. An album's sequence is a journey, and songs benefit by being placed at a certain point along the way.

However, 'Trenches' does not need such help. Matt and Time exchange vocals line-by-line, with the trademark chorus, perfect. Tim's guitar work is on the money, and the breakdown section – stripped down to percussion and rolling bass – is one of the band's more-experimental early moments. The opening discordant riff jumps in and out tremendously.

In a way, the subject matter is quite heartwarming. Tim spent time in the underworld of squats, and with fellow street punks, looking out at the glass skyscrapers. And he watched on as friends moved out of the squats, off the streets, into houses of their own. Yet Tim stayed put. The lyric suggests he likes it that way: another pointer towards his union with this way of life. He was doing okay in the trenches.

Some of my friends moved on a domestic simple life
They're all gone a few of us remain
Only few of us want to keep it the same
I got it right out in the trenches tonight

'Holiday Sunrise' (Armstrong, Freeman)

A track hinting at the sound of future Rancid albums. Together with 'Detroit', it's this album's most commercial-sounding track – a big strong chorus, easy-to-decipher verses, textured backing vocals and a nice melodic guitar riff: the kind you can sing along to – all packed into 1:45, in the key of G major. Yet the lyric is very much based on life on the street and how hard it is, again. Life on the street on Christmas Eve, ain't easy, as indicated in the lyric. In fact, it's as hard as it can be. And it contains one of Tim's most heartbreaking lines: 'I cried when I had no shoes/'Til I met the man with no feet'. Makes you think. Makes you cry. Makes you reconsider.

'Unwritten Rules' (Armstrong, Freeman)

Matt takes the lead vocal. 'Unwritten Rules' is a break from the heavy and dark subject matter basically present throughout the album. The unity of the punk rock movement, the unity of going to a show, drinking beer and experiencing loud live music – something we all love, so why not write songs about it?

Rancid wrote more songs along these lines as time passed; unity pushed further by reaching out to the classes: 'I'm gonna amplify the rage of a class that's thought inferior/The message in the volume, this song's a carrier'.

'Union Blood' (Armstrong, Freeman)

I love a hidden track. 'Train In Vain' wasn't listed on earlier vinyl copies of The Clash's *London Calling*. And 'Union Blood' is not listed on the sleeve of *Rancid* either. I have no idea why – a deliberate mischievous oversight or a genuine error? It creates an air of mystery, either way. But what a track. And speaking of The Clash, 'Union Blood' is the track here most reminiscent of them: a constant comparison, as the years were to reveal.

There's a history lesson in the lyric. 1933 saw a five-day strike in San Francisco in response to the sacking of four dockworkers for wearing union badges. The result was the reinstatement of the workers. The union leader Harry Bridges led the protest. Rancid immortalised Bridges in the later song 'Harry Bridges' too. In my opinion, 'Union Blood' is one of Rancid's most underrated and overlooked numbers. But then again, I love The Clash, remember.

'Get Out Of My Way' (Eric Dinnwitty, Eric Raider)

The album closes with its only cover song. Influential North California ska band The Uptones originally wrote and recorded 'Get Out Of My Way' – their 2 Tone mod version quite at odds with Rancid's ferocious punked-up interpretation. Tim was a huge fan of 2 Tone.

It's a great album closer. Not only is it a storming performance of a great song, but the lyric kind of sets the tone for what will follow. The message is, no matter what, we will do what we do, so fuck you – get out of our way. There's a determination in the performance; Rancid would be back, meaning business, in the very near future.

It works on a macro and micro level. There's reference to those who attend shows but tell others how to behave:

Who do you think you are?
Do you think you're some kinda cop?
Why did you come along?
Get Out Of My Way!

It also references society: 'I don't want your lies/I don't want your rat race/Get out of my way!'.

All ingredients of the band's early work are on board: lightning-busy bass, aerosol-can guitar and snarled, slurred, growling vocals.

Rancid represented a crescendo of rage and gave us a trunkload of promise.

Radio Radio Radio (7" EP) (1993)

Personnel:
Tim Armstrong: guitar, lead vocals
Matt Freeman: bass, vocals
Lars Frederiksen: guitar, vocals
Brett Read: drums, vocals
Label: Fat Wreck Chords
Producer: Donnell Cameron
Release date: US: 26 August 1993, UK: N/A
Running time: 7:57

1993 was a huge year for the band. They became a four-piece, beefing the sound up in the process, giving their sound more flexibility and variation. However, Billie Joe Armstrong of Green Day was never in the band, contrary to some rumours. Matt Freeman explained to *Cult Of George* Fanzine in 2018: 'Billie Joe was hanging around, and we asked him if he wanted to play a show with us. He came to a practise and said 'Sure'. So, he played the show, but of course, he couldn't play in the band, 'cause he's in Green Day, so we got Lars'.

The band continued their recruitment campaign, quickly centring on a Californian: Lars Frederiksen, born Lars Dapello. Lars took his mother's birth name, to distance himself from his father after his parents divorced. Like Matt and Tim, Lars came from a broken home, and was raised by his mother from the age of three. With his heavily working-class credentials, he appeared cut from the very same cloth as Matt and Tim. Lars' CV included English punk heroes U.K. Subs. Having worked alongside legendary singer Charlie Harper, Lars would bring the kind of grit and experience gained from performing with such a warrior. UK audiences are different to those in the United States, and just by spending time with the Subs, Lars soaked up the London influence of Camden Town and The Clash, Soho and The Sex Pistols, and the 2 Tone from the Midlands. Lars' appeal was obvious – a huge enigmatic and engaging character, superb guitar player, songwriter, and strong vocalist. Furthermore, he looked cool: spiky punk-rock hair and tattoos. He would bring substantial character to the band. And crucially, The Clash, Stiff Little Fingers and Ramones were all quartets. This is the perfect balance in a punk band: two guitars, backing vocals and a solid rhythm section. Rancid would look cooler in photographs also.

Lars had finished his stint with U.K. Subs by the time Tim approached him at Gilman. He pushed a tape of Rancid's material at Lars, which he learnt back-to-front by the time he showed up his for the first practice. Lars told *Hitlist* in 2012: 'This is what I've been waiting for my whole life. Everybody wanted to be fucking Fugazi: all those fucking emo kids. There were no punk rockers anymore'.

However, a familiar issue soon reared its head. When Lars was asked to join Rancid, Tim asked him if he drank. Just a few beers after the show, was the reply. This means different things to different people, however, and sure enough, after a show, Lars got truly pissed. Tim recalled the episode in the 2012 *Hitlist* interview, stating, 'He was fucking annihilated'. Matt immediately wanted him out. But Tim had a heart-to-heart with Lars, and an ultimatum was given. If Lars got drunk one more time, he was out of the band. Lars never drank again. Tim even threatened to drop his gear off at Togo's (a sandwich shop where Lars used to work) if Lars had one more beer. Lars kept his end of the bargain, and so did Rancid.

Lars's personality was big, tough and thick-skinned. Any problems would be dealt with if he was around, and the other three loved it. Early shows saw them unite quickly, as a tight, powerful unit. Brett's work improved even more, and they relied less on Matt's dexterity to fill out the sound. And, importantly, the band's brotherhood grew.

Next up was a product. Once again, Rancid headed for Donnell Cameron at Westbeach Studios. The result was an EP. *Radio Radio Radio* is a bullet of a 7" – four tracks, two each side, totalling just under eight minutes. Tim took the lead vocal on each cut. It was released on vinyl only: Rancid's only release on Fat Mike's (NOFX) Fat Wreck Chords. It was issued on 26 August 1993: just three months after the band's debut LP.

I spoke earlier of how good Rancid now looked in photographs. Like The Clash, there was no single point of focus: all four band members had their own individuality. The cover photo for *Radio Radio Radio* (taken by Jesse Fischer) illustrates this, with Lars in the foreground. The EP saw the band's new spray-stencilled logo appear for the first time.

Musically it was still high-octane punk rock: a continuation of *Rancid*. But significantly, the songs on side one were both re-recorded, improved and included on the band's second album.

Side One
'Radio' (Armstrong, Freeman, Armstrong)
This hugely important Rancid song still regularly opens the band's shows. It's a true anthem and the song that drew me in many years ago. The lyrics, I feel, were written directly for me, with the references to how music gives people a place to go – away from all hassles, all addictions, all worries. It takes me away from what I know I must do tomorrow, or what I wished I had or hadn't done today. I'm sure many other people feel the same way. Music is salvation. 'For when the music hit, I feel no pain at all'.

Compared to the version included on *Let's Go* – the band's second album, released the following year – it has a work-in-progress feel. The production is raw, and lyrics are duplicated from one verse to another. They are hard to decipher at times. It's a high-velocity performance, but the song's obvious melody, still flies high – it's not buried too far below layers of attitude, defiance and feedback, to be audible: an important point. The arrangement is also vastly different. There's no triumphant chanting of 'When I got the music, I got a place to go' at the end. It draws to a very sudden halt. The backing vocals are more crafted and show more guile.

The song was co-written with Billie Joe Armstrong of Green Day. By including references to songs by The Clash ('Radio Clash', 'The Magnificent Seven'), they got the likes of myself onside. Here was a song by a band that recognised and promoted the heritage of the music. That meant something to me. The song is also very personal to Tim. There are clear references to his Dad: how he never gave Tim the love he craved, so he had to look elsewhere. Booze is obviously one answer, but the triumphant discovery of the power of music won the day. An amazingly prophetic and autobiographical piece of work.

'Dope Sick Girl' (Armstrong, Freeman)
The second track on side one, and another one re-recorded for the *Let's Go* album. This time, however, the version is similar with only subtle differences. The production is again raw, and this is the main difference from the more polished *Let's Go* version. It's the record's most significant track. The song is melodic and is a significant change in the band's sound. The arrangement lets the song breathe and allows a hell of a lot of craft. It's more structured, and not just a high-speed punk workout. It has hooks galore, vocal and six-string, in the key of G-major. It also displays Lars' guitar work – the melodic riff an indication of what would follow in the future.

Tim's words are a street story about love for his girl. But his girl uses this love to steal his money to obtain drugs. He still loves her despite this. The song's theme is loathing for drugs and what they make people do. It's very sad, and rather than blame the girl, he blames the dope. 'This song is about a girl/Who ripped me off/She was dope sick'.

'Just A Felling' (Armstrong, Freeman)
Side two of the EP is more in keeping with the band's debut album – high-octane and furious – and hilariously and intriguingly, contains tracks which have misspelt titles. 'Just A Felling' is in fact 'Just A Feeling'. The track was included on the band's 2007 *B Sides And C Sides* compilation, and on the 2008 *Fat Music For Fat People* collection: both times listed as 'Just A Feeling'!

It's a blistering track, splattered with Lars' guitar blasts, egged on by Tim ('Go on Lars, hit it!'), almost as if introducing the new boy to the fans. The band's backing-vocal arrangements were now more balanced and showed a lot more finesse: a trait that was to become a band trademark.

'Some Ones Gunna Die' (Fisher, Howe, McLennan, Miller)
A significant inclusion. The decision was made to cover a UK band's work for the first time. Not only that but a true underground band: Blitz, from Derbyshire, England. Blitz recorded the song in 1981 as the lead track for their classic *All Out Attack* EP.

   With its 'Oi! Oi! Oi!' chorus chants and melodic suspended riff, it's a true UK street-punk classic; a rabble-rousing number with a direct prophetic lyric about football hooliganism, tribes and after-match shenanigans. Rancid perform a faithful – if sped-up – version of the song. Nidge from Blitz told *Punk And Oi* in a July 2005 interview: 'Lars sent me a copy of Rancid doing 'Someone's Gonna Die', but I thought it was played too fast. I told him it was different'. Nidge's words confirm Rancid couldn't spell, too!

Let's Go (LP) (1994)

Personnel:
Tim Armstrong, Lars Frederiksen: guitar, vocals
Matt Freeman: bass, vocals
Brett Reed: drums
Producer: Brett Gurewitz
Recorded at Fantasy Studios, Berkeley
Label: Epitaph
Release date: 21 June 1994
Chart positions: US: 97, UK: Did not chart
Running time: 44:23

In 1994, the musical landscape was plateauing. The glossy big-haired 1980s rock had long since given way to the more-earthy sounds of grunge and pop-punk. Both genres were under the punk umbrella, maybe, but were not *punk* enough for some. Generally, grunge had a lot of self-loathing lyric content, and pop-punk had a bubblegum quality which didn't appeal to punks brought up on the likes of The Exploited and Anti-Nowhere League. The spirit of punk wasn't truly represented. Defiance seemed to be lacking, replaced by a sulky acceptance of fate: whether personal, social, emotional or political. There was little fight. And there were only so many songs about masturbation, depression or lost love, that punks could tolerate. Nor were there many spiky hairdos, tattoos or studded biker jackets around. We needed someone who could inject that proud, truculent street spirit back into the scene. Step forward Rancid – for a while in the 1990s, the last true punk band standing.

This really began with the release of their second LP *Let's Go*. The band were already on the way to becoming a well-oiled, efficient machine. The new more-beefy sound gave the quartet real power. The backing vocals were full and had a contemporary edge and clarity. The second guitar gave more melody amidst the velocity. Lars had also given the band a splattering of colour. His musicianship could hold its own next to Matt's virtuosity, and Lars was one hell of a songwriter, to boot. Being part of the worldwide punk network via U.K. Subs, also helped get Rancid out to a wider audience. Tim told *Hitlist* in 2012: 'When we started, we were below the radar. But then Lars was in the band, and the record (*Let's Go*) came out on Epitaph, and we started getting a lot more attention'.

Rancid were very much a punk band, and *Let's Go* is very much a punk record. It doesn't vary too much, tonally. It's high-speed: 23 bullet songs fired in about 40 minutes. However, there were developments. Firstly, the production. The sound has more sheen. It's still raw and gritty but is easier on the ear. It presented the music in a way that enabled it to mix with the new alternative world. It was recorded in Matt and Tim's hometown of Berkeley, at the legendary Fantasy Studios where Green Day's *Dookie* – and even Europe's *The Final Countdown* – were recorded. Brett Gurewitz was in the producer's chair. It was mixed at Westbeach Studios, where the band's earlier material had been recorded.

Secondly, songwriting. Tim's lyrics were becoming more and more evocative, moving away slightly from urban blight and more into storytelling and commentary. Thus, they encompassed more subjects and attracted a wider audience. The roots were very much on the street, but the metaphors and symbolism went much further afield.

Whilst 95 per cent were tracks that could've been included on any of the three previous releases, there was one number that seemed destined to make its mark beyond the punk network. 'Salvation' was a punk track with distorted guts all over it. But its slower tempo, crowd-pleasing chorus and easily distinguishable vocals, made it the first Rancid song to connect with the mainstream music masses. In the process, 'Salvation' helped *Let's Go* amass some half a million sales. The Recording Industry Association of America certified it Gold in 2000.

Let's Go was released on vinyl, compact disc and cassette. Early vinyl copies featured two 10" records with the 23 tracks spread across four sides; very nice, especially as it was pressed on white vinyl. Its red cover art incorporated a map of the Bay Area, with a clenched fist above the title. It seemed like a call to arms. Tim knew it was time to take his band beyond its cosy underworld home. The back cover photograph is legendary – spiky Lars and Tim giving the bird, flanking Brett and Matt who are sitting in a motor. With the now-customary range of gig flyers and song lyrics included on the inside, it seemed the complete, defiant punk package.

'Nihilism' (Armstrong, Freeman)

Leaping out of the traps at breakneck speed with a barrage of 'Hey"s, 'Nihilism''s opening seconds shared characteristics with 'Adina': the first track on *Rancid*. The introduction is even reminiscent of 'Someday' by Operation Ivy. But 'Nihilism' has a much more crafted, fuller and stronger sound.

Fans get their first taste of Lars Frederiksen as a lead vocalist: he takes the opening lines in the verses. With his immense presence in the song's video, Lars' arrival – spiky mohawk an' all – was well-and-truly announced. The lyric even references his home turf of Campbell:

> Come into union district
> Drive down on Sharmon Palms
> White ghettos paint a picture
> Broken homes and broken bones

It's a great song, featured in many fans' top-three Rancid song lists. It's a positive message, nd is a terrific example of Tim's evolution as a wordsmith. The word 'nihilism' means nothingness: a pointless existence. The lyric deals with the desire to get beyond this and have a purpose; to remove it as a philosophical obstacle. Look at these lines at the end of the verse: 'Nihilistic feelin's are movin'/If I try really hard, you'll see right through them'.

Nihilism was also a secret society among Russian communists. If you incorporate this leftist notion, the song has even more depth. Ivan Turgenev influenced the society, and had a role in the abolition of serfdom, incidentally – an achievement the working-class warrior Tim would applaud. Of course, both Tim and Lars had struggled with alcoholism. Nihilism can be its result, or its cause, or both. Despite nihilism being the philosophical state of nothingness, it is something from which society can build. *Lives* can also be built from it. It's punk rock's duty to be positive. So, marrying the two, makes perfect sense for Rancid.

'Nihilism' remains a regular in Rancid's setlist.

'Radio' (Armstrong, Freeman, Armstrong)

This early Rancid signature song was covered in depth during the *Radio Radio Radio* chapter. However, this is the definitive version, with production sheen from Brett Gurewitz, and a new arrangement including an extended end section with the triumphant chants over the D/F#/G chords. The arrangement is more crafted, and the lyrics are decipherable: the latter point, is crucial, given their quality.

'Sidekick' (Armstrong, Freeman)

The Wolverine song. Tim, like so many, was a comic-book fan when he was young. 'Sidekick' is about a dream he had where he joined Wolverine from the movie *X-Men* and went around kicking bad guys. These included *X-Men* character Senator Kelly, governments, authorities, criminals and drug dealers. All exploit people on the streets, as do the police, who evict folks just wanting a roof over their heads.

> Do not bill abandoned buildings
> It's nice to sleep when you've got a ceiling
> Neighbourhood watch say we gotta put a stop
> Can't have people livin' for free, call the cops

Tim spent time in a squat, of course. All are given the boot by Wolverine and his sidekick Tim: *a lesser-known character*. The lyrics check Oakland and West Grand – places in the Bay Area, where people live and benefit from volunteer projects: which then got closed by SWAT teams. These teams deserve a kicking too, according to the lyric.

Musically it's a whirlwind. It speeds off like a rocket boost, with light and shade in the verses and choruses, respectively. Again, a more-sophisticated arrangement.

'Salvation' (Armstrong, Freeman)

The song that took the band away from the tight-knit punk underworld to the big wide world of music stardom. It was the album's second single lifted for radio airplay, and MTV heavily rotated its video. The black and white film featured Lars and Tim as partners in crime, running from the authorities, eventually finding sanctuary with Matt and Brett: to paraphrase the lyric, rats on a mission. There was also footage of the band squeezed into a tiny room, performing the song.

'Salvation' reached number 21 in the *Billboard* Modern Rock chart. And with it, Rancid made their first big breakthrough into the mainstream. The track was subsequently featured in the pilot episode of *Buffy the Vampire Slayer*.

Tim explained on the band's *Myspace* site in 2009: ''Salvation' was the last song written at the very end of making *Let's Go*. So, when we feel something, we go with it'.

It was easily the band's slowest song to this point. Tim's voice is fantastic; the words easily audible. The question-and-answer chorus, works incredibly well, drenched in ringing, overdriven guitar; with a nice guitar break to allow a breath of air. The defiant lyrics, document Tim's time working for the Salvation Army, with an angry tirade at rich people tucked away in their palaces in Blackhawk, California, which is close to Oakland. They live pampered lives, whilst the poor suffer and exist on the kind of handouts Tim and his co-workers were distributing. Tim later said 'Salvation' was genuinely the only song he wrote in anger.

I can't believe these people live like kings
Hidden estates and diamond rings
I'm a rat out on a mission
I'm in your front yard, under suspicion

'Tenderloin' (Armstrong, Freeman)

A welcome return to Matt's lead vocals. It's a very *street* lyric, about a prostitute in the Tenderloin area of San Francisco, with Larkin mentioned in the second verse. Larkin Street is the street where hookers and their clients congregate. The words are very positive, turning the scales on society's view of prostitution. The verse lyric contains the giveaway line, 'The tricks she gets them, she's not a victim'. 'Tenderloin' is in awe of a very self-assured woman: knowing what she's doing and why. The chorus raises my blood temperature: the thing I like most in music. Matt's rolling bass line is immense, with Lars' lead guitar breaks duelling with the bass to great effect. I've always considered this as a Matt song, due to the dominance his booming voice gives it.

'Let's Go' (Armstrong, Freeman)

A blistering title track, and an easily relatable lyric: anyone – whatever your situation – gets pissed off with the same old aggravation, people, bosses and frustrations of everyday life. How about we do something about it? Let's go, let's escape. That's what this one's about. Positivity. The chorus tells you all you need to know

Let's Go! Where the shores are green!
Let's Go! Where the music's loud!
Let's Go! Where there 'ain't no problems
Fuck this, fuckin' transit

The message is, *Do something about your situation*. Curiously, it's the one track where the lyric is not included in the artwork. All the other songs have their words printed as part of the sleeve.

'As One' (Armstrong, Freeman)
The influence of Operation Ivy is apparent in this lyric. Clocking in at just 94 seconds, 'As One' is a clear call for unity of people of all creeds, tribes and races. It's a clear extension of the Op Ivy classic 'Unity'. Again, for a punk track, it has a strong multifaceted arrangement, over a simple A/E/D chord structure. The thick, rich backing vocals are stunning. They shine like a spiritual beacon.

'Burn' (Armstrong, Freeman, Raider)
Co-written with Eric Raider from The Uptones. It's a busy number with loads going on – a gritty avant-garde opening, lightning bass runs and tons of light and shade. It's an angry number, this characteristic accentuated by expletives and Tim's snarling chorus.

The theme is that America cannot keep stamping on populations, whether they are native to the land prior to the union, or an overseas territory. The verse lyric shows a violent 1960s protest element: 'Thirteen red and white stripes flying/White for skin and red for dying'. And the chorus: 'We don't need no water/Let the motherfucker burn'. The track is an example of the evolution in Tim's lyrics. No longer were they merely tales of urban blight. This is more global. This is anti-oppression; anti-racism. Furthermore, US troops used to chant the above line after bombing raids in Baghdad. 'Burn' is very much against the symbol of the American flag when it's used to justify such acts.

'The Ballad of Jimmy and Johnny' (Armstrong, Freeman)
Jimmy is also mentioned as a character in the title track and returns here with Johnny, where they represent two different kinds of skinhead. Scene politics is the subject matter, with Jimmy the traditional, original skinhead who loves ska and the gritty, rough sound of 1969 reggae: Trojan. Johnny is a boot-boy-style skinhead, loving the Oi! sound of Last Resort and the like. There are plenty of references to the lifestyle stereotypes: for example, Jimmy's scooter, his ska-loving girlfriend, and Johnny's macho gas-guzzling pickup. Stereotypes maybe, but this division in the skin scene has led to violent issues on both sides of the Atlantic. As ever, the lyric is not only a commentary but a plea for unity based around the basic question: What the fuck were they thinking? As is often the case in scene politics, the problems are pathetic. Why can't we just get along??

'Gunshot' (Armstrong, Freeman)

This has a wonderful psychobilly backbeat, with tasty Brian Setzer-esque guitar licks. The pace never really lets up, and the high-speed rock-'n'-roll tempo and the key of C provide a good variation from the earlier out-and-out punk feel. Matt takes the lead vocal on the one-dimensional lyric focussing on heartache. Sometimes someone hurts you so bad, it's like a gunshot to your heart. It's a simple rock-'n'-roll number, really, with a stomping sound to match: all done-and-dusted in 1:51, but a favourite track, that the band have always played deep into their set, often as part of the encore.

'I Am the One' (Armstrong, Freeman)

Religion is the subject, nicely balancing the lighter theme of 'Gunshot'. Even this song's opening seems to have an evangelical light, the title being chanted as if at the top of Mount Sinai, surrounded by beacons of light. The backing vocals are constant, and at times complex. It's not quite like a full choir but is certainly full-on and rich.

The theme has anti-religious connotations. It's deep, suggesting strongly that religion is more important in lives than the people who live them – to the extent that the actual suicide of a kid, becomes secondary. The pressure the kid feels from his religion, is immense, and his suicide is taken as a sin, punishable in the afterlife.

> Bleeding at the gates I can't come in
> Courage that abates a life of sin
> Sure that it holds and it holds no others
> With the lies of the brave and the kid don't matter

A heart-breaking and deep song, cleverly disguised in its complex arrangement.

'Gave It Away' (Armstrong, Freeman)

A brilliant band performance, with plenty of hooks and opportunities to shine, taken up. Lars' single-string guitar melody – country-blues in feel – skips along and is light on its feet, allowing Tim's gritty and soulful vocal delivery to hit the mark. Again, the pace is unrelenting, Matt's bass full of technique with its treble pops. Brett again somehow makes the whole thing swing. Though this is a punk album with no real experimentation, the psychobilly influence appears more than once. The lyric is not as deep and layered, and this suits the tune. It's over in a flash: 71 seconds in fact and over half of that is spent singing the title in the chorus, with two verses telling a tale of giving a heart and loyalty to someone who then gives it away and moves on.

'Ghetto Box' (Armstrong, Freeman)

This track, again, highlights the band's increasingly exciting vocal arrangements, with Tim hurling in short sharp lines, with the group responding equally sharply as a backing-vocal unit. Matt takes the chorus lead vocal. Urban blight influences the lyric, with tension in every line; drugs, robbery and gangland. Defiance against authority, and right-wing bullying police tactics are given an appropriate response in the verses: 'Nazi Cops fuck you!/Attack on the backstreets with you'. 'Nazi cops fuck you' is a familiar punk war cry. Punks ain't gonna stop. Punks will be defiant to the last, especially when it comes to fascist police.

'Harry Bridges' (Armstrong, Freeman)
One of the band's – and particularly Tim's – finest moments. A slower track, very meaningful. Harry Bridges, the subject of 'Union Blood' – the unlisted track from the band's debut album – returns. The song has a punk folk protest feel, with simple arrangements and root-note musicianship.

Harry Bridges was a 1930s union leader who campaigned on behalf of dockworkers' working conditions. His actions caused a general strike, and police killed three workers at a gathering in support of the strike. Harry Bridges marched the three bodies to their funerals a few days later and passed the police ranks, who warned him against doing so. The media tried to discredit him by labelling him a communist. Tim articulates this in the song's first half, giving us a history lesson. He then creates the fictional character Eddie, who worked in the motor industry. Eddie then lost his job, then his wife and self-esteem: like what happened to many workers over time. Eddie is a metaphor for those workers, particularly for those in the Californian docking industry in the 1930s. Industry bosses time-and-time-again let their workers down. 'Over and over again the doors are locked, and the windows are broken'.

'Black And Blue' (Armstrong, Freeman)
A hard-hitting track, as the title suggests. Matt's lead vocals have always given Rancid albums good balance. It's catchy too: a tune that stays in your head for a week after you've heard it just once. It's in key of G-major. It also has plenty of fun in it and is still played live regularly to this day.

'Sedation through a nation/Intoxication of a generation'. The theme suggests a whole generation is unaware of what's going on around them, as they're intoxicated by materialism. It sanitises life, meaning populations miss what's important so long as they can take a trip to the mall and buy stuff. They are beaten black and blue by their blindness.

Tim's off-mic and provocative 'Yeah, whatchya gonna do' is very Joe Strummer-esque. Joe often sang seemingly throwaway lines in The Clash whilst Mick Jones took the lead.

'St. Mary' (Armstrong, Freeman, Frederiksen)
This is a real standout, as it represents Lars' first full lead vocal performance for Rancid. It's one of his early co-writes too, and immediately he grabs the

opportunity and rises to the occasion: something he's done ever since. His big clear voice is different to Tim's slurred, gravelly delivery. Tim takes the bridge vocal.

'St. Mary' is full of sharp hooks, with every second made to count. There's bursting Chuck Berry-esque solo guitar work, and again a rock-'n'- roll smack rhythm provides the backbeat.

It's yet another good example of storytelling, with Mary being a woman whose partner was shot by the police. Now she's out for revenge

Mary's out the door with a loaded 44 in her hand
Shooting down the law that shot down her dear departed man

Self-explanatory – with a reference to Salinas: one of California's most crime-ridden cities.

'Dope Sick Girl' (Armstrong, Freeman)
The same song and arrangement as on the *Radio Radio Radio* EP, but re recorded and brightened up.

'International Cover-Up' (Armstrong, Freeman)
You know how you thought our governments hide things rather than fix problems in the first place? Well, that's the point of this song, written from the perspectives of external observers and compatriots.

Musically, it's brimming – anarcho-punk anger merged with light and shade, provided by guitars dropping out completely at the end of the verse. Tim sings the line 'You don't know what it's like' over a virtually naked backing. Again, there's blistering lead-guitar work, and full-on, big, loud backing vocals. Matt Freeman's bass runs and breaks are speedy and fluent, but his playing isn't given such a high profile on *this album*, as the band became better at their craft.

'Solidarity' (Armstrong, Freeman)
This has a chorus with its word content crammed right on in, almost to the point of overload. 'Solidarity' is ambitious and very open-to-interpretation. The regular Rancid themes of unity and togetherness are obvious, but failure to get anywhere near this, can be catastrophic. It can result in suicide, murder or revenge-killing. Then the whole thing can be in a second. Killing only takes this long: whether suicidal or homicidal. Profound stuff.

'Midnight' (Armstrong, Freeman)
An easy song to miss out on, sequenced deep in the album. However, it's a hidden gem. It has question-and-answer verses and great terrace-style chorus vocals allowing Tim's lead vocal to wander. Again, it's Joe Strummer-esque. It's

little wonder the likes of me responded to this new band in the early-1990s: we'd been desperate for a new incarnation of The Clash.

The pace of the album at this point is top gear: no pause for breath. 'Midnight' has a great, close, hypnotic and intermittent rock-'n'-roll guitar lick over a C/F/G structure, played as if it's looped. The theme of urban blight reappears – in truth it's never that far away. But the overriding message here is the familiar one of defiance, and as a result, 'Midnight' is very punk.

'Motorcycle Ride' (Armstrong, Freeman)

There are hypnotic riffs here too. It's a belting psychobilly number with a rock-'n'-roll high-school vibe. Matt leads the chorus with his distinctive growl, and Tim spits out the verse with snarling cool. It's all over in under 80 seconds.

It's well worth making sure you pay attention to these tracks deep down in the running order. This one is simply fantastic – a punk rock song made to enjoy at maximum volume, to take away all your worries: preferably on vinyl. It gets my blood temperature up, good and proper. On top of that, the words in verse two's second half are very familiar. For the uninitiated, they were taken lock-stock-and-barrel into the mighty 'Time Bomb': one of Rancid's biggest tracks, released just a year later.

> If you want to make a move, then you better come in
> It's just the ability to reason that seems so thin
> Living and dying and the stories that are true
> The secret to a good life is knowing when you're through

'Name' (Armstrong, Freeman, Dinn)

There's a real old-school UK street-punk feel to the album's penultimate track. The shouty Oi!-style chorus is real fist-in-the-air stuff – Tim's gritty vocal its ideal foil. He's accusing almost anyone in the angry chorus: 'You! Don't! Know my name/You don't know my name'. It's a relatable theme, about anonymity at work, at school and in society; about not feeling valued and being merely a commodity. It's credited as being co-written with Eric Dinn (aka Dinnwitty) from The Uptones.

Over time it's become a bit of a cheap and tired music-journalist trait to compare Rancid to The Clash. In my view, this is obviously a compliment, but there's so much more to Rancid. Their continued experimentation alongside a constant barrage of proper punk records over the years is at odds with The Clash: who only made one true punk-rock-sounding album. That said, there is an obvious influence on 'Name': it could easily have sat alongside 'What's My Name' on that seminal Clash debut.

'7 Years Down' (Armstrong, Freeman)

The album's final track, and one the band very rarely played live. The reason may be in the theme's very personal nature. Tim's words focus on struggles with addiction and recovery. It is quite literal. The achievement of recovery comes through. 'House' refers to a detox facility in Richmond, California, where Tim spent time before the Salvation Army days.

> There's a place I like to go
> When I got no food or I got no shelter
> It's a house where I can get away
> For maybe three days
> To get off the drink and stay off the haze

His time here and with the Salvation Army were key moments in Tim's life – the point from which his humility and recovery really began. The word 'salvation' is so appropriate, and of course is the title of the band's breakthrough single. It's the very seed from which the Rancid root germinated, and *Let's Go* can be seen as the first full-size leaf on the tree.

'Salvation' (Single) (Armstrong, Freeman)
Release date: US: 1994, Chart position: US: 21
A promo CD single was issued in the US only. It was the same version as on the album. It was the band's breakthrough hit and remained on the *Billboard* chart for 15 weeks.

...And Out Come the Wolves (LP) (1995)

Personnel:
Tim Armstrong, Lars Frederiksen: guitar, vocals
Matt Freeman: bass, vocals
Brett Reed: drums
Label: Epitaph
ProduceR: Jerry Finn, Rancid
Release date: 22 August 1995
Chart positions: US: 45, UK: 55
Running time: 50:25

Steadily increasing sales of *Let's Go* over six months, together with heavy MTV rotation of 'Salvation', began to suggest the band may have had what it takes, and that the public at large had an appetite for raw, abrasive music, as long as that music had tunes. *Let's Go* had some, but Tim had many more up his sleeve. As Rancid went into 1995, they were hungry, lean, bursting with ideas, and ready to take everybody on. They wanted to do the best they could in the studio and on stage.

The band's spiky visual was suddenly in vogue. Two years previously it would've been turned away by every disc jockey and TV presenter. Tim and Lars' often-brightly-coloured mohawk cuts looked fantastic on MTV: especially in grainy black-and-white footage, oddly enough.

Let's Go was certified gold. The East Bay – once the radical-left faction of Californian punk – was now a shrine for expensively-suited, greedy major-label A&R representatives. *Dookie* had thrown Green Day into the stratosphere, and Rancid's labelmates The Offspring, followed. Those reps were looking for the next big thing. Matt reminisced in 2012 that 'We were the perfect target to get caught in the crossfire'. Billie Joe Armstrong stressed how much Operation Ivy influenced him, and two members of that band were in Rancid. Matt Freeman's words were spot-on. The sharks started circling.

Just before Christmas 1994, it looked as though Rancid were about to *do a Clash*, and sign to a major. The *Los Angeles Times* reported that Epic Records tabled a contract worth $1,500,000, with a publishing deal on top worth a further $500,000. The band maintain they never agreed to any such deal, but the fact they were even *speaking* to Epic, was too much for some members of the punk police and their fraternity. Matt told *Hitlist* in 2012: 'We got made to feel that we were evil for even talking to these fucking people'. Tim went into greater detail:

> Ever since I started playing punk rock, people have said major labels are shit. When I was a kid, people would tell me, 'Oh don't fucking drink, man, it's bad for you', or 'Don't do drugs'. But I gotta have my ass kicked before I'm gonna really believe any of that. I'm so fucking glad we stayed on Epitaph.

Throughout the history of punk, bands had signed to major labels. Sex Pistols seemingly released singles with as many majors as they could before settling on Virgin; The Clash controversially signed to CBS in time to release their debut LP, and of course, Green Day were on a major by the end of 1994. Furthermore, pop queen Madonna was keen on Rancid: so-much-so that she wanted them to sign to her Maverick label. Bizarrely, she allegedly even sent a nude picture of herself to the boys to lure them. It didn't work. Rancid stayed with Brett Gurewitz at *Epitaph*. Thank God. Brett Gurewitz and Rancid were indisputable kindred spirits. Let's move on.

The Epic affair gave the band new inspiration. New song 'The 11th Hour' documented the whole episode candidly. And the title of their next album was a definite slap to those who criticised the band for talking to Epic. The phrase comes from author Jim Carroll, who makes an appearance on the album. All will be revealed shortly.

Rancid's third album ...*And Out Come The Wolves* will from hereon be referred to as *Wolves*. What an album. It proudly takes its place high on the list of the best punk albums of all time, alongside the likes of Ramones' debut and The Clash's *London Calling*. The Clash comparison is once again inevitable. *London Calling* is an experimental record. Stylistically it embraces rockabilly, ska, rock, reggae, pop and even a Phil Spector-esque wall of sound. No *London Calling* tracks sounded like the bolshie, distorted, shouty punk of The Clash's debut. But even though *Wolves* is experimental compared to Rancid's first two albums, it doesn't jump all over the place like *London Calling*. Nor does it ditch Rancid's original punk sound. They remained loyal to those fans who loved them for this.

Tim and Matt were totally justified in bringing in the ska elements on *Wolves*: they invented the ska-punk genre after all. The ska elements certainly gave *Wolves* a new twist, as did the use of Hammond organ and the scratching of DJ Disk (real name Luis Quintanilla: a San Francisco turntablist). Here lies the experimentation on *Wolves*. *Wolves* is chock-full of killer melodies, backed up with ferocity, hooks, ability and accessibility. The songs are more crafted, often slower in tempo. But nonetheless, it's most definitely a punk album; totally identifiable as being by the band who made *Let's Go*. Matt explained to *Rolling Stone* in 1995: 'I think the third record is a quintessential Rancid record in a lot of ways, just because the four of us really gelled as a band. We've grown up, we play better now, and I think that's what came out on this record'.

The recording locations were significant. Rancid utilised Fantasy Studios in Berkeley again, and, for a lot of the lead vocals, the infamous Electric Lady in New York City. Brett Gurewitz recorded the band in NYC where the album was mixed. New York's punk edge seeped into the album. In my mind, this contributed to the nature of the tracks. Some 40 tracks were recorded in the album sessions: eventually whittled down to the 19 that made the final cut. Production was taken on by Jerry Finn, and Rancid themselves. The band were becoming more and more confident in their skin, and knew exactly how the record should sound: a supreme step. Brett Gurewitz helped in New York as if keeping an eye on things.

All songs were co-written by Tim, Lars and Matt – again significant: this shared responsibility and recognition further embedded Lars as a member. Unity. Brotherhood. Friendship.

The LP's iconic artwork was devised by Jesse Fischer, Gina Davis and Lint (Tim Armstrong). Jesse also took the photographs, which included shots of the NYC skyline, and the 52nd-and-Broadway junction, immortalised in 'Olympia WA.'. The front cover shot of a mohawk punk was in fact a photo of Lars from June 1995 in downtown L.A.: taken with Jesse's Hasselblad 503cx on a Tri-x film, with strobes. It's a classic punk image, matching Pennie Smith's famous shot of Paul Simonon smashing his Fender bass on the cover of *London Calling*. What many may not realise is that Tim scrawled the phrase '...And Out Come The Wolves'. The band's spray-stencilled logo was now firmly in place, and this all helped with identity. And *Wolves* gave Rancid their first UK chart entry.

'Maxwell Murder' (Armstrong, Freeman, Frederiksen)

As with the first two records, the opener is short and sharp. Lars takes the vocal. The band manage to squeeze so much into 85 seconds – killer verses, chorus, and that unbelievable bass solo. Yes, a bass solo. In the first track. Plus, there's an excerpt from the Lech Kowalski film *Gringo*. 'Maxwell Murder' works harder and quicker than almost any track I've ever heard.

Theories differ about the song's subject matter. Some maintain it's about the death in mysterious circumstances of Robert Maxwell: the British media tycoon who in the early-1990s, fell from his yacht and drowned. The reference to the UK emergency dial code 999, led some down this path. But that's a bit of a ridiculous conclusion – Maxwell died overseas off his yacht (allegedly): 999 would not be dialled anyway. 'Dial 999 if you really want the truth/He ain't Jack The Ripper, he's an ordinary crook'. The emergency number would be dialled to shop a dealer (in this case Maxwell) if a junkie wanted to get past induced hell and live a real-life away from the nightmare that addiction brings. Maxwell was a street kid who sold drugs right outside Tim and Brett's crash pad in Berkeley. Maxwell basically *murdered* people with his *cure*.

> Maxwell got a hand in this plan
> He knows you are in this plan
> Shop the rock before you bought it
> Sickness Maxwell knows you caught it

In 1995, Tim told *Rolling Stone* about the song's theme, and about Maxwell: 'He's got the cure for people man, you can see it in my face'.

'The 11th Hour' (Armstrong, Freeman, Frederiksen)

Pete Townshend-style staccato C/F/G chords open one of Rancid's most important songs. The theme was mentioned earlier. It really was the 11th hour when Rancid decided to stay with Epitaph and not sign to Epic. In even talking to a major, they were risking everything. Friendships were going to disappear. 'The face of isolation/Well, that's one you recognise'. The key is in knowing where the decisions – and therefore the real power – lies. It ultimately, of course, lies 'with you'. It was up to Rancid to stay with Epitaph and Brett Gurewitz, realising who their real mates were, in the process. Epic could've taken all of this away, just as an addict puts trust in a dealer. This analogy is never far away in Tim's words. The third verse is almost euphoric:

I was almost over, my world was almost gone
In a sudden rush I could almost touch the things I done wrong
My jungle's made of concrete, and through silence I could feel
Oh my aim is true, and I will walk on through these mountains made of steel

The subtle tap of Bashiri Johnson's bongos, the growth in the guitars' power and the glorious elation of the backing vocals, combine, as Tim's words grow from a whisper to a triumphant scream. It's almost spiritual and is recognisable to anyone who has ever almost gone the wrong way only to make the right call at the 11th hour.

'Roots Radicals' (Armstrong, Freeman, Frederiksen)

We're in the zone now. This was the album's first single. Lars opens with a tale of his bus ride from Berkeley to downtown Campbell and mentions his buddy Ben Zanotto, who tragically died after an overdose. Tim follows with the second verse telling us about his own journey south from Albany: which sounds like a hell of a lot of fun, by the way. These vocal interchanges tell everyday stories of characters, tunes, drinking and bus rides – the kind we all took as teenagers, to meet mates, drink, party, shoplift, listen to music, whatever – with a list of characters including the legendary Zanotto, Tim's friend Rude Girl Carol, and all the punk rockers and moon stompers; indirectly, Desmond Dekker too, of course.

The galvanising chorus is the ultimate in a punk rock-gig sing-along. The song is feisty as fuck. By the time we reach the end of the guitar solo, it sounds like the whole thing is about to take off. I've heard 'Roots Radicals' sound great around a campfire, ram the dance floor in a steaming club, and crooned by a sultry, sexy singer. It's simply a fantastic track, in the truest tradition. There isn't much that gets me as pumped as this. Furthermore, it strikes a chord with Jamaican icon Jimmy Cliff. He recorded his own track called 'Roots Radical': a different song altogether. Rancid performed a version of Cliff's 'The Harder They Come' at the Tibetan Freedom Concert in 1997, and Tim later produced Cliff's 2008 album *Rebirth*. Rancid performed 'Roots Radicals' live with 'Ruby Soho', on *Saturday Night Live* in November 1995.

I used to put on shows in my hometown of Leicester. There was a kids punk group called Kid Vicious (Geddit..?), and the singer Jack used to do a solo acoustic version of 'Roots Radicals'. The C/F/G chords suited him. He was about 12 years old. To inspire a kid on the other side of the ocean to get into punk rock so young and do a version of your song, is the ultimate. Tim, Matt, Lars and Brett – you should be proud. Jack – I hope you're doing okay and still listening to Rancid.

'Time Bomb' (Armstrong, Freeman, Frederiksen)

This gritty anthem is one of Rancid's best-known numbers and was the album's second single. It was used in the 1995 Jim Carrey film *Fun With Dick And Jane*, in an episode of *Gilmore Girls* in 2000, and even as the entrance music for UFC fighter Antonio Banuelos. Its video was directed by Marcus Raboy, whose work includes videos for Shakira, Santana and Luther Vandross. In all, 'Time Bomb' was probably the number that propelled Rancid near the top of mainstream music.

The influence of Tim and Matt's previous band Operation Ivy, came to the fore on 'Time Bomb', as did Tim's love of 2 Tone and reggae. It's tight as fuck, with snappy up-tempo reggae rhymes, and Tim spitting out the storytelling with swagger. Matt's bass cuts a deep dub groove, the guitar lick is clean, and the chorus drops neatly into place. It's very light on its feet. A Hammond organ solo owns the breakdown section and is played by The Uptones' Paul Jackson.

The song is said to be about Eric Hogan, who set up and owned American Graffiti Tattoo. Eric was also a member of the Hells Angels but was ultimately murdered by one of their number for allegedly sleeping with another member's wife. The final verse describes his demise:

In tears come from the razor that's been tattooed below his eye
His mother cries she knows he's strong enough to die
He's rollin' in the Cadillac, it's midnight, the roof is down
Three shots rung out, the hero's dead, the new King is crowned

The lyric tells the life of a hustler. Tim cleverly interweaves the two subjects. Some of the verse was previous included in 'Motorcycle Ride' from *Let's Go* (See the entry in the previous chapter).

'Olympia WA.' (Armstrong, Freeman, Frederiksen)

The amazing opening quintet is completed by this much-loved track. Following four of the band's most famous tracks ain't easy, but this hook-laden gem lives up to the task, no problem. It has a guitar riff in the key of G that you can sing, and the chorus is one of Rancid's biggest, and that's saying something. The New York City references are ever-popular – the 52nd and Broadway line immortalised not only in the song itself but in Jesse Fischer's cover photograph. Indeed, for a period, Lars and Tim considered living in the city, due to its edge and punk rock scene.

However, this is a sad lyric. At the time, Tim had a relationship with Tobi Vail of Bikini Kill. It's reasonable to assume that much of this is about her:

It gets all too demanding, she's all gone and I'm stranded
Something burning deep inside of me
All I know is that it's 4 o'clock and she ain't never showed up
And I watched a thousand people go home from work

Tobi and Bikini Kill herald from Olympia, Washington.

Lars and Tim's friendship saves the day, as Tim is stood up his girl in the city that never sleeps. Lars is there for him. Fortunately, so are three Puerto Rican girls ready to take them to the funhouse. I think I would too, given the circumstances. Ultimately, despite all the attractions of New York City, all Tim wants to do is get back home. It's lonely being surrounded by people but not the person you want. It's all in the chorus.

'Lock, Step & Gone' (Armstrong, Freeman, Frederiksen)

Following the epic sounds of the previous numbers, we get a return to ballsy punk rock; all rough riffin' guitar with awesome backing vocals. Tim and Lars' lead vocal exchanges have real attack, and the song's arrangement shows how rapidly the band had become craft experts. It's one of my favourite live songs, incidentally.

The theme is of tough backstreets, where by taking a wrong turn you could get done over by a street gang. Street gangs, drug dealing kids; whoever – urban blight once more, balancing out the personal experience and fables of the opening five tunes.

'Junkie Man' (Armstrong, Freeman, Frederiksen)

A little more experimentation. It's amazing what can be done with just two guitar chords (A and D). The eerie riff sets an ethereal feel. A town's crazy man – shunned by the population – is the central point. He sits on the sidewalk, randomly barking out his feelings. The rest all head to the other side of the street. However, this guy has his own story. Shouldn't we hear it? This includes junkies. When they're out of it, the rest give them a wide birth. But again, they have their story.

'Junkie Man' is a reflective song with an uncomfortable lyric. But it's catchy, lively and fast-moving. It's full of hooks, and the vocal interchanges are again fabulous. Tim does the verse, Lars the bridge; they both do the chorus. Magic.

Tim invited *The Basketball Diaries* author Jim Carroll to write a poem for *Wolves*. Carroll did just that and performs the poem just before the third verse, probably just where a guitar solo world normally be. It includes the line 'and out come the wolves' just as the chords change. It's a transcendental moment, perfectly timed to maximise the final verse's impact. The band's acquaintance with Carroll was accidental. He was in New York recording an interview for his film *People Who Died*, upstairs while the band were putting finishing touches on the *Wolves* vocals. The band met him and asked if he'd sing on the album. After hearing 'Junkie Man' just once, he wrote the lyrics and recorded them in one take.

Furthermore, 'Junkie Man' features the scratching of DJ Disk. A significant inclusion, linking the Rancid's street punk to the urban sound of dance music.

UK ska band Death of Guitar Pop covered 'Junkie Man' on their 2021 *Pukka Sounds* album. It's given a 2 Tone workout. Tim is a huge 2 Tone fan of course, and the lineage between Rancid and Death of Guitar Pop, mirrors that of Rancid and late-1970s England. The fact it gets passed *on*, shows the power of music. Death Of Guitar Pop are Rancid fans, incidentally.

'Listed M.I.A.' (Armstrong, Freeman, Frederiksen)

Another straight-down-the-line rocker, like 'Lock, Step & Gone'. It's riffy, with no fat on it at all (Is there on any Rancid track?). It's a great singing performance from Lars: the phrasing on the opening verse lines being particularly effective.

The theme is the feeling you get when you arrive in a narrow-minded town with people treating you like shit. This is often based on nothing but your appearance. Many a punk rocker or radical would recognise the sentiment behind lines such as these: 'God damn it man, I almost had it/Threw me out the door and called me a faggot'. At 2:23 in length, it's one of the band's longer punk numbers.

'Ruby Soho' (Armstrong, Freeman, Frederiksen)

A huge number, the album's third single, and one of the poppiest-sounding tracks in the band's repertoire. But no worries – when songs are this good, nothing else matters. It's another example of Rancid stretching themselves musically. It still has a punk edge, but wasn't punk enough for many of the band's early fans. However, no band can develop and evolve if they remain a one-trick pony. Again, it was a song written right at the end of making the album, like 'Salvation'.

The use of light and shade is one of track's strongest features. The chorus is enormous: like a hurricane. It's so loud. The sombre, spacious verse allows the story to unfold, which has two parts to it. The first is that of the narrator and his loneliness. The second part involves the couple in the next room. The narrator provides a commentary on the arguments next door, clearly heard through the bedroom wall:

He's singin' and she's there to lend a hand
He's seen his name on the marquee, but she will never understand

The couple's relationship cannot work, because the man is going to be away touring with his rock band. The man in the relationship – according to many – is Matt Freeman. He and his girlfriend of five years – Kathy – broke up as Rancid started making it big. Matt has confirmed this in interviews through the years, though he had no idea he was part of the storyline at the time. Other theories are that the song is about the ending of one of Tim's relationships. However, given Matt's acknowledgement, the former seems more likely. As for the identity of Ruby Soho, this is a phrase, person or place being used as a metaphor for where the band's path lay: 'Destination unknown/Ruby Ruby Ruby Ruby Soho'.

At a televised live performance in Cannes, the band did an impressive version. Tim of course sings the verse and then skips to the back of the stage dancing away to himself, whilst Matt and Lars roar out the words full of masculine testosterone. Brilliant.

The track was a hit, an MTV favourite, and even reached 13 on the *Billboard* Modern Rock chart. To this day it often closes the band's show or main set.

'Daly City Train' (Armstrong, Freeman, Frederiksen)
A punchy ska stomper. Its precise rhythm is augmented by another Matt Freeman deep-bass groove, with melodic guitar licks skipping things along, giving it a biting edge. The cleaner tones underline that there is more to Rancid than gutsy punk rock.

The track features the character Jackyl from 'Rats In The Hallway' on *Rancid*. As Tim's lyric is based on actual life experience, Jackyl was most probably somebody close to the band. Rumours over time have suggested some of Jackyl's traits are shared with Jesse from Operation Ivy. Daly City is in the East Bay.

The message is clear. You can still be imprisoned even though you're not locked up – it's the choice you make of how you live your life. Being true to yourself is the only real way. Jackyl lived his life according to these principles.

Jackyl was one of the ones that perished
Yeah he was one of the ones that was already saved

'Journey To The End Of The East Bay' (Armstrong, Freeman, Frederiksen)
A personal, sentimental lyric about Operation Ivy and their part in the Gilman scene. Thus, it's one of Rancid's epics. The chorus is typically huge, and the arrangement displays backing-vocal dexterity. The lyric doesn't glorify Op Ivy, but focuses on friendships within, and how the band attempted to make things work. The song is candid about their foolishness and how unwanted attention led to their demise. It also touches on being let down by others, particularly those who exploited the Gilman scene. The lyric's are very direct, don't need interpretation, and have tragic charm.

Started in '87 ended in '89
Got a garage and we'll play anytime
It was just the four of us, yeah the core of us
Too much attention unavoidably destroyed us

'She's Automatic' (Armstrong, Freeman, Frederiksen)

After the experimentation and epic sound of the previous three cuts, 'She's Automatic' performs another neat balancing act. It's a hard-rockin' no-nonsense workout which reminds us we have a gritty, tough, street, punk-rock band operating at full throttle. Thus, the *Wolves* sequence is stabilised. Lars takes full charge, with a commanding, powerful lead vocal performance – something he does so well, dominating the riffing guitars, the booming, busy bass and pounding drum skins: the reason I love punk rock music. The lyric is straightforward, about a woman who is a goddess. No messing lyric, no messing music.

The track has been a mainstay of their setlists.

'Old Friend' (Armstrong, Freeman, Frederiksen)

Ska once more, and a poignant number. The lyrics are possibly Tim's most poetic, retaining the sad tone represented across much of the album. The theme is the band's rising star and the effect of this on relationships, friends, partners and family. Relationships are tested by the loneliness of being out on the road, and the temptation of drugs is always 'round the corner. In Cleveland – the lyric's location – it all becomes too much:

There must be something about you that I liked
But right here in the rain it just don't seem right
I always go out, I never hide
But in Cleveland I should've stayed inside
The unfortunate get preyed on by vulture's eyes
86 cents in these pockets of mine
You can take my money, you can take my time
But you can't take my heart, it's in the city behind

Mention must be made of the instrumentation. The tight groove is nailed as ever by Matt's bass and Brett's locked rhythm. But the combination of slick, melodic guitar runs and Hammond-organ fills, is majestic: the latter provided once more by Paul Jackson. The chord progression is standard (A/E/F#m/D), but there's a reason it's often utilised – the same sequence – or a variation on it – is also used in classics like 'No Woman No Cry' and 'Let It Be'.

'Disorder And Disarray' (Armstrong, Freeman, Frederiksen)

Another crunching return to punk rock. It's high-octane, with emphasis on the word 'crucify' – being put out to dry by record companies encouraging a band to sacrifice their roots in order to make millions. Of course, in selling so many records, many accused Rancid of selling out. However, the spirit of punk is not to be constrictive, it's the liberty to do exactly what you want. Anyone who wants you to do exactly what *they* want you to do, is just not getting the point. The subject matter here is slimy label reps hooking-in bands, signing them (crucifying them), and running off to do the same to the next victim – reminiscent of the Gilman scene breaking up, and the near-miss Rancid had with Epic.

'The Wars End' (Armstrong, Freeman, Frederiksen)
Very relatable – leaving home to find your true self, following your true path, and not just doing what's expected of you. The character is Sammy. Tim's words tell the story perfectly. I love the reference to Billy Bragg and his left-wing politics: something Sammy's mum was clearly uncomfortable with.

> Little Sammy was a punk rocker
> You know his mother never understand him
> Went into his room and smashed his Billy Bragg record
> Didn't want him to hear that communist lecture

The message to Sammy is, *Don't worry kid, it'll get better. Be true to yourself.* This punk ballad is patriotic to its cause and is a flag-waver, Lars leading the way with a fantastic lead vocal. He's a great troubadour, and this song has great connection, live. Furthermore, he's also always been a big Billy Bragg fan, famously covering 'To Have And Have Not' with Lars Frederiksen And The Bastards.

'You Don't Care Nuthin'' (Armstrong, Freeman, Frederiksen)
The album's balance is retained with another punk-rock banger. It's one of the best vocal performances from Tim and in particular Lars: their passionate fiery exchanges working incredibly well. Jenny Demilo is the subject of the song, or rather is on the receiving end of the lyric attack. It's savage stuff. Demilo was an infamous scene figure, clearly someone Tim needed to get out of his system.

> Hey girl, you better please take a look around
> Explore your heart and find out for yourself
> Jenny Demilo
> You don't care nuthin' about me

It's a tasty verse backing, using A-minor and F chords, lifting off in the chorus: cracking stuff.

'As Wicked' (Armstrong, Freeman, Frederiksen)
A favourite song of mine. Tim's lead vocal is packed with character in every syllable: even the 'na-na-na-na-nas' after the second chorus. A warmly distorted

51

and melodic guitar riff reminiscent of street-punk bands like Cockney Rejects and Cock Sparrer, backs the verse, with another inevitable huge chorus pouncing like a jaguar: classic ingredients.

It's another poignant lyric, loaded with empathy, hence the passion and soul in Tim's singing. Tim and Lars knew about life on the street; all four band members came from broken homes and saw plenty they didn't want to see – a young woman on the street with a friend lying dead nearby; an old boy searching in a litter bin for something to eat: this is what's wrong, what's wicked in the world. It's reflective stuff, Rancid sticking up for those at the bottom of the ladder: people with nothing to their name but the street on which they roam.

'Alleyways And Avenues' (Armstrong, Freeman, Frederiksen)

Quality deep cuts make a band stand out from the competition. Rancid have them in spades. If the quality remains high across the whole album, the listener stays on board. In return, the band get loyalty. This song is a prime example of a classic deep-cut and represents quality sequencing with only a minor pause for breath after 'As Wicked'. This attention to detail is so important.

It's a tune much-loved among Rancid fans, with its 'Oi oi oi' street cry prior to each chorus, raising the roof in concert halls. It is a slower number, but is very intense, with Tim's restrained vocal, full of soul. The terrace chant of the chorus is spine-tingling. Once more, Rancid achieve the holy grail in raising blood temperatures with their music, making the hairs on the back of my neck stand right up.

The slower tempo suits the lyric's subject matter of social issues, conflict and inequality. The lyrics are easy to follow and decipher, which is important when dealing with such a crucial theme. There's no use singing about this when no one can understand what the fuck you're on about. It is poetic, and in typical fashion, there's a positive spin: 'I'm a battering ram comin' through to you/In every alleyway and avenue'. The battering ram that is unity, can smash social injustice if given the chance. As Joe Strummer said: Without people, you are nothing. The lyric promotes unity, and unity is what Rancid are all about.

> I figured out the problem, yeah the problem is you
> You didn't see us comin' and now there's nuthin' you can do
> He's a different colour but we're the same kid
> I will treat me like his brother, he will treat me like his

'The Way I Feel' (Armstrong, Freeman, Frederiksen)

Final tracks on albums *must* be good. They can't just make up the numbers. This rip-roaring, feisty-but-crafted finale sums up the band's evolution to this point. The melodies were stronger, the themes more personal, and the performance, basically, was better. This is the sound of a band in top form, confident in its skin.

The lyric is open to interpretation. It can be taken as the story of a breakup, whether it be a relationship or friendship; a kind of *You've changed, that's why we're breaking up* kind of theme, like many songs before and many since. However, it may be interpreted as a comment about the bands from the punk scene who had signed to majors, especially when one considers Rancid's own sensitivity to the criticism they received.

You move up the ladder at very rapid speed
We moved methodically and calmly
When you get to the top, you see enemies
You say that I'm different, you say that I'm different
The only thing different is the way I feel about you

Defiant, eh? Rancid were all very aware of their position in the punk network. They wrote songs about real situations, many of which found their way onto one of the greatest punk-rock records of all time. The reality of the pedestal they were inadvertently climbing to, would not have been lost on Tim.

Contemporary Releases
'Roots Radicals'/'I Wanna Riot' (7", CD single)
Release date: US: 1994, Chart position: US: 27
This was released by Epitaph on 7" vinyl and compact disc, and as a promo. Though there was no UK release, a further version was issued in Australia in 1994, which also featured 'Salvation' from *Let's Go*. The single was released in conjunction with Epitaph, on Cortex Records: a sub-label of Shock Records.

A-side
'Roots Radicals' (Armstrong, Freeman, Frederiksen)
This is different from the album version, marginally. The arrangement is the same, but the recording is, if anything, even more alive and thrilling: it's unbelievable to think that would be possible really. Seriously, this is as good as punk rock music gets.

B-side
'I Wanna Riot' (Armstrong, Freeman, Frederiksen)
Razor-sharp guitar lines set the tone for this gritty, storming ska stomper. It's also on the 2007 *B Sides and C Sides* compilation, 2012's *Essentials*, and the *All The Moon Stompers* 2015 collection. The 'Oi' chants are fantastic, and the chorus is a winner. It's brilliant live. 'Oh! Yeah! I Wanna Riot!'. With a chorus like that, it was always going to be a winner with skins, moon stompers and punks alike. Tim takes the lead vocal, his gargle hard to decipher at times, but Strummer-esque in its effect: a compliment, of course.

'Time Bomb'/'The Wars End'/'Blast 'Em' (7", CD single)
Release date: 1995, Chart positions: US: 8, UK: 56

A-side
'Time Bomb' (Armstrong, Freeman, Frederiksen)
Same version as on the album. Rancid's highest-charting UK single to date.

B-side
'The Wars End' (Armstrong, Freeman, Frederiksen)
Same as on the album.

'Blast 'Em' (Armstrong, Freeman, Frederiksen)
A cracking punk song. It opens with a machine-gun-rattle of a riff. It has a steady quick tempo (but not high-octane) with a driving, chugging, thrashy verse riff and a typically gritty vocal performance from Tim. The chorus has the vocals going back and forth in the mix, staccato style.

The lyric's protagonist is frustrated and may well take this out on anyone who crosses him, so watch out – like 'Travis Bickle', which later appeared on the *Indestructible* album.

It has great energy, and the fact it's tucked away on a B-side is a shame in some ways, but it's a proper good reward for anyone who buys 7" singles. It was later mopped up on the *B-Sides And C-Sides* and *Essentials* compilations.

'Ruby Soho'/'That's Entertainment'/'Disorder and Disarray' (7", CD single)
Release date: 1995, Chart Positions: US: 13. UK: Did not chart

This was released on Epitaph in most territories, with assistance from Cortex in Australia and Semaphore in Germany. It's a nice sleeve, depicting a DIY drawing of a girl with a big city skyline behind her, by none other than Operation Ivy vocalist Jesse Michaels.

A-side
'Ruby Soho' (Armstrong, Freeman, Frederiksen)
The album version.

B-side
'That's Entertainment' (Armstrong, Freeman, Frederiksen)
This is not a cover of The Jam song of the same name but is 90 seconds of punk rock traditional street-style, and its super-speed sound could even have appeared on *Rancid*. The lyric – about time spent at a liquor store passing as entertainment – would've fit right in amidst the urban blight. The lyrics are

indecipherable at times, but a simple punk chorus is something I love, and always will: 'I say, it's only entertainment, Ya-yeaaahh'.

'Disorder And Disarray' (Armstrong, Freeman, Frederiksen)
Same as the album version.

'Olympia WA.' (Armstrong, Freeman, Frederiksen)
Release Date: 1996. Chart position: Did not chart
This was a CD promo issue in the US only, and was the album recording.

...And Out Come the Wolves (Expanded edition) (2015)
An expanded version of *Wolves* was issued in most territories and included 'That's Entertainment' and 'Blast 'Em' as bonus cuts.

Life Won't Wait (LP) (1998)

Personnel:
Tim Armstrong, Lars Frederiksen: Guitar, vocals
Matt Freeman: bass, vocals
Brett Reed: drums
Label: Epitaph
Producers: Tim Armstrong, Lars Frederiksen
Release date: 30 June 1998
Chart positions: US: 35, UK: 32
Running time: 64:12

Can four Oakland, California, natives with ridiculous mohawks make a better record than *London Calling*? Hard to believe, but with their third CD ...*And Out Come the Wolves* (Epitaph), Rancid does just that, one-upping the British group by moving beyond brute-force punk without forfeiting urgency.

These words were taken from Chuck Eddy's review of *Wolves* in *Entertainment Weekly* in 1995. Many concurred, of course, and *Wolves* sold. And sold. To date, it has racked-up sales well in excess of 1,000,000, and it went platinum in the United States and gold in Australia and Canada. The impact it had on a whole generation of young punk rockers cannot be understated. People wanted to dress like Tim, wanted their hair spiky like Lars, and were inspired by the band's focus and spirit. These young lions had now joined the iconic figures of the first punk rock wave, and Rancid roared on behalf of 1990s punk kids.

Rancid could play their instruments. Music is better if the instruments are played right, *see*. Kids followed their lead, the result being that very few decent and influential bands in the 1990s carried that early punk characteristic of hardly being able to play instruments. The ballsy, bolshie and catchy punk sound, was back. The melodic and catchy hooks ensured accessibility the world over. MTV lapped up the big tracks on *Wolves*. On Rancid's post-Covid 2021 tour, songs from *Wolves* still made up a big chunk of the setlist.

Back in 1997 however – after extensive touring – Rancid had to decide what to do next. How the hell could they follow up *Wolves*? Would they go back to their angry punk roots, to maintain credibility with old school punks? Or would they churn out another rugged hook-laden album to please those fans they'd amassed with *Wolves*, or even tap into more contemporary sounds?

The temptation to experiment further was not something they could resist. *Wolves* was the sound of a band beginning to peep around musical corners to stretch their capabilities. The next album would see them sprinting 'round these corners, and then dashing down every other alleyway and avenue to look for more. The result was an album full of pop, left-field post punk, rockabilly, ska, roots reggae, spacious dub and even Trinidadian calypso and Jamaican mento: balanced with slices of traditional punk, mind. However, it wasn't just a desire to try out new styles that was influencing the band. Three years of touring had taken them all over the world, and this was a huge factor in how 1998's *Life Won't Wait* came out. The album will be referred to as *Life* from now on.

It was recorded in several locations – Los Angeles, San Francisco, New York, New Orleans and Kingston, Jamaica. When quizzed why by Modern Rock radio in 1998, Tim explained: ''Cause that's what we had done before. It would have been easy to lock ourselves up and bang out a record. We'd rather fly by the seat of our pants and kinda experiment everywhere. We get different vibes from different places'.

The studios used in L.A., were Sunset Sound, Ocean Way, Bloodclot, Brooklyn, Record Plant and The Complex; in New Orleans: American Sector and Kingston Penthouse. In New York City, Coyote and The Site were used; in Kingston Jamaica, Waterhouse. This long list really underlines the band's seat of their pants approach to making a record, to paraphrase Tim. But it would result in Rancid spreading their wings musically, socially and politically. This couldn't be achieved by staying in a San Francisco or New York studio, only venturing out for sodas and subs.

Life also had a huge cast of guest musicians, including dancehall reggae superstar Buju Banton, members of The Specials, NYC ska supremos The Slackers, and Hepcat, just for starters. The album's lyrics reflected Rancid's travels and subsequent worldview. Themes were no longer confined to urban blight and personal tales, but dealt with Yugoslavian suffering and Polish riots, alongside scene politics and American hypocrisy. Lars told *Rolling Stone* magazine in 1998: 'I think this is our most political record by far. I think we just got a broader spectrum. We've been to a lot of different places and see different sides of things'.

Away from Rancid, both Tim and Lars managed to get married amidst all of this. Tim married singer Brodie Dally from The Distillers, who he met when she was just 16 years old. Lars tied the knot with Megan.

Work on *Life* began with barely a breath taken after the *Wolves* tours. Upon its release, reviews were favourable. MTV stated in 1998: 'If Rancid are not known as pioneers at this stage of their career, they are still master craftsmen. Their new album, the band's fourth, should solidify that reputation'.

Others, such as Permanent Records in LA, picked up on the band's broadening horizons: '*Life Won't Wait* reveals a wizened Rancid that's done some travelling and seen some shit'. Lars viewed the inevitable comparison to The Clash's experimental opus *Sandinista* as nothing but positive: 'Being compared to The Clash is like – if you're a ballplayer – being compared to Willie Mays. So that's nothing but flattering. Just being used in the same sentence is really nice'.

Rancid wanted their records to be as good as possible. Tim and Lars decided to share production duties on the album. Again, seat of their pants. Songwriting duties were spread out, but interestingly, Tim wrote a large chunk of the album on his own. As I said earlier, Rancid never released a bad album.

Their quality and consistency are to be admired throughout, and this certainly applies to *Life:* their most experimental of albums.

Life Won't Wait was released on compact disc, vinyl and cassette. Some gorgeous orange-vinyl gatefold-sleeved double albums were available on release. Artwork was again by Jesse Fischer, who also took the photographs, which matched the album's challenging themes by being more artistic and interpretative. It wasn't an obvious punk sleeve as before, and for all intents and purposes could've been the cover of an R.E.M. or Pixies album. However, Rancid's spray-stencilled logo was still there. This is Rancid after all, and there's something reassuring in that they remain rooted on the same gritty real-life street, no matter where that street is.

'Intro' (Armstrong)
We are used to Rancid albums opening with a short sharp attack. However, the opener here is more like an advisory piece – 48 seconds of off-the-rails punk rock, tottering along a precipice, as frantic as it is ferocious. It has wild distorted harmonica blowing across the top, courtesy of Lester Butler, and comes complete with a commentary containing the following warning: 'The phenomena you are about to witness could well revolutionise your way of thinking'.

You've been warned.

'Bloodclot' (Armstrong, Frederiksen)
The album's lead track and second single is familiar Rancid. It has a big chorus with 'Hey-ho' chants as a hook, and big strong vocals. Lars takes the lead. Tim's casual response in the question-and-answer verses, facilitates a set of brilliant vocal exchanges. Loud, distorted guitars rock throughout, breaking down after two minutes, to a funky break using a riff (F/Bb chords) similar to the one late on The Rolling Stones' classic 'Can't You Hear Me Knocking'. Brett's performance shows a drummer doing so much more than keeping up with Matt and Tim.

The lyric is about making no apology for believing in yourself. Lee 'Scratch' Perry is referenced in the opening line.

Well, I'm a crazy upsetter (Driving me insane)
Yeah I'm a streetwise professor (Who am I to blame?)
Now if you listen to the record (Do you feel the same?)
Well, it don't get any better (Going backwards again)

Ramones are obviously referenced with the 'Hey-ho' chants. And the backing vocalists on those chants? – Marky Ramone, Howie Pyro (The Blessed, D Generation), Tim Shaw, Kristen Krisapline.

'Hoover Street' (Armstrong)
Vocal assistance is provided here by Greg Lee and Alex Desert, and piano by Eric Stefani. It's one of the tracks recorded at Waterhouse, in Kingston, Jamaica.

Just as anyone is getting comfortable, along comes this experimental quirk. It starts out breezy enough, with warm, distorted guitar chords. But then it drops into a sparse rimshot rhythm, in D-minor, with Tim's whispered words on top – which are stretched out for over a minute before the chorus comes crashing in (briefly). Then we're back into another lengthy verse, with xylophone pings sitting with brief guitar bursts. Usually, Rancid race to the first chorus. The chorus – when it arrives – consists of two words: 'Oh yeah'. It's usually a positive statement, but here it's mournful: not surprising given the lyric's theme. The chorus is also reminiscent of Junior Byles's 'I Got A Feeling' from the classic *Beat Down Babylon* opus – a definite example of Jamaican influence

'Hoover Street' references glass pipes used to smoke or snort crack. It presents characters looking to escape their drug-dominated lives in El Salvador and seek life in the promised land of the United States. But there they fall into the same drug and alcohol habits as in their homeland, only this time under the shadow of a gleaming, expensive Los Angeles skyscraper. Hoover Street is in L.A., in a notorious gang and criminal neighbourhood. The brother (Mario) gets murdered on the street, and his sister is alone in a new country. The description of Mario's demise is striking:

Now see poor Mario
He caught a hot one through the lung
Now he's done, so God bless the man

'Hoover' Street is a significant song, showing the kind of articulation Tim was becoming capable of – likewise the music backing, which moves with the story, and creates an uncomfortable and claustrophobic sonic, matching the lyric.

'Black Lung' (Armstrong)

This track has a definite left-field twist, with a discordant guitar riff and a more-complex rhythmic structure. Cleaned up a bit, it could've been by Gang of Four. Stripped down a bit, it could have been on *Rancid*.

The theme is unmistakably Tim. The subject is coal miners and how their union bosses would get in bed with their employers, exploiting the very workers they were supposed to protect. And what's left for the miner – his face and lungs blackened with coal dust? To look forward to the bell or whistle at five o'clock, signifying the end of his working day. The mere sound of the riff – though very punk rock – suggests the frustrating theme.

Sign a petition under working conditions
Union is in bed with coal operators (call of Berettas)
Carry freedom looking for something
To get your family better life for every single day
Some things keep me going
I got no one to blame

Five o'clock is coming
Do you feel the same when a lonely whistle calls out your name?

The words are a further example of Tim taking the side of workers. 'Union Blood' from *Rancid* is another example, as is 'Harry Bridges' on *Let's Go*. It would develop further over time.

'Life Won't Wait' (Armstrong, Frederiksen, Vic Ruggiero, Buju Banton)

A huge number, one where the band truly do fuse differing music cultures and style. Vic Ruggiero – from New York's finest: The Slackers – plays keyboards, and the track was recorded in Kingston. In the 1990s, 'Life Won't Wait' was an intense live experience.

The ska influence on *Wolves* wasn't a surprise, given the Operation Ivy heritage. Here though, Rancid went much further, with a boss reggae groove straight from 1969. It sounds deep, with a bass note that hits you right at the back of your knees. It struts, and the C-minor key is slightly sinister. This is combined with 1970s roots-reggae lyric consciousness, about methods the authorities employed to control populations: 'Division is the new world order'. By ensuring populations remain divided – by race, social class, sex – governments make it easier for themselves. If society spends time fighting amongst itself, then it's unlikely to rise against its leaders. Authority likes to put itself in the role of preaching unity, but does the opposite, as Lars told *Rolling Stone* in 1995: 'It's about how they keep us fighting each other. Blacks and whites, who's really fighting each other, who's in control'.

Rancid are about unity. This stretches back to Op Ivy with 'Unity', and Tim pleads for it in many of his lyrics. The religious references take the song to a deeper level. Religion is to blame for so much trouble and violence all over the world – dividing populations, creating hunger, causing soldiers to fight overseas against people they have no personal quarrel with: 'The conscience of the public cannot be put to sleep'.

Buju Banton makes his presence felt, big-time. Rancid repaid the favour by contributing to 'Misty Days' from the man's 1999 album *Dubbing With The Banton*. His toasting adds credibility to this Jamaican-influenced number. His lengthy monologue accentuates the point. His Jamaican tones, masterfully deliver the lyric, despite some fan reaction that his verse was at times unintelligible. Tim responded to these comments in *Lollipop* magazine in 1998: 'Like an old dancehall record. Listen to a B-Man record, tell me what he's sayin'. You gotta listen to that kid a bunch of times, then you can understand it'. Incidentally, as with Jim Carroll on *Wolves*, the meeting of Buju and Rancid was apparently accidental, literally on the streets of Kingston shortly after the band arrived there to record 'Life Won't Wait'.

Ultimately, Rancid can be rightly proud of this cut. Reggae music by punk bands is rarely as well-crafted as this.

'New Dress' (Armstrong, Frederiksen)

An almost Springsteen-esque rocker. The backing is skilfully played, and quite subtle insofar as the guitars are clean compared to the heavily distorted kind that dominated the band's catalogue to this point. And it's political – this time focusing on the early-1990s Yugoslav war, and the troubles in Northern Ireland. Humanity is at the centre. People still live lives, or try to, as civil war, rages. A girl still wants to look her best: new dress and all. And she pleads to the West – especially President Bill Clinton – to help her and her country out:

> Yugoslavia's been blown to bits
> She got a new dress
> She's looking to the West
> Entertain the idea of peace on Earth

It's one of the band's poignant moments. One measure of an artist is the ability to provide comment without preaching. This war protest song does exactly that. It's a brilliant vocal performance by Lars, incidentally: big, powerful and full of character.

'Warsaw' (Armstrong)

Back in the early-1990s, it was a comparatively short journey from the former Yugoslavia to Poland. On 13 December 1981, the Polish government declared martial law in Warsaw, and arrested all trade union leaders except for Lech Walesa. Riots broke out as a result, many rioters using baseball bats to smash up a discotheque. These baseball bats were sold to them by the United States years before, in order to promote baseball in Poland! Walesa of course, would later become Poland's leader as the communist walls came tumbling down.

'Warsaw' is the second number that – to my ears – could've been included on one of the band's early releases. It's high-octane, with a big chorus that's easy to raise your fist to. Poland's Solidarity movement had posters similar to Rancid's artwork: something not lost on the band, I'm sure.

'Hooligans' (Armstrong, Frederiksen, Vic Ruggiero)

From world politics to street politics. In fact, a return to the scene politics between rival skinhead factions: rude boys (hooligans) versus boot boys. It's similar subject matter to 'The Ballad of Jimmy And Johnny' from *Let's Go*, but this time the thing is on a mob level.

> Well, The hooligans and boot boys know one thing for sure
> Scars been stricken on their face

The Specials' Roddy Byers aka Roddy Radiation lends his instantly-recognisable guitar-playing to the track. His clear-but-cutting melodic playing appears as the track starts and is a constant presence. He even comes close to stealing the show.

It's an up-tempo slice of ska that's very light on its feet. Neville Staples – the self-styled original rude boy – and The Specials' Lynval Golding, help on backing vocals. For Tim – a huge 2 Tone fan – this must've felt like heaven. Staples' cries of 'Rancid!' towards the end are wonderful.

This was the album's first single and is one of several tracks co-written with Vic Ruggiero of The Slackers. It's a great lead vocal by Lars once again.

'Crane Fist' (Armstrong, Frederiksen)

Recorded in Waterhouse, Jamaica, this is the first of four songs in entirely different genres. 'Crane Fist' is stomping, heavy dub. Lars' lead vocal has attack and is ferocious, which doesn't always go with the subtle, pure beauty of the dub genre. Tim balances it with his vocal interjections. Rancid remain true to themselves but use a melodic bass-heavy riff to drive the track: a technique utilised in reggae. Furthermore, the mix uses vocal snatches, guitar chimes, percussion dropouts and shuddering piano (Vic Ruggiero) to build the cut. Tim grabs the mic, and toasts halfway through, before Lars delivers the final verse.

The lyric addresses the inevitable life of crime many are destined to live, as evidenced in the chorus:

Oh no
Some people live illegal
All their lives are led in evil

'Crane Fist' comes with four long, full verses and Tim's lengthy toasting monologue. The spirit of rebel music – in both punk and reggae – is in its honesty and its defiance. Reggae verse needs listening to properly, in order to understand it. It's worth the effort.

'Leicester Square' (Armstrong, Frederiksen)

A song that could've appeared on *Wolves*. In this rocker, the Springsteen vibe is again clear. It's full of hooks, riffy guitar and passionate vocals; sharp, short and snappy, to boot; street-themed, hinting at urban blight. On *Life,* urban blight is international: in this case *en route* from the US to London. It's a tough life on the streets, and people get broken. The main character Michael is involved in gang life, and basically, fights, punches and drinks his way through the streets on both sides of the Atlantic. He's a cold, virtually numb character. It's the way he's ended up living his life. Fists come first, thoughts later, if at all. It's called survival.

'Backslide' (Armstrong)

This is possibly the biggest surprise on the LP. It's very northern soul in feel. Tim's vocal is loaded with soul, showing once more that there's more to his singing than punk-rock grit.

The horns are courtesy of David Hillyard (The Slackers, David Hillyard and the Rocksteady Seven), Jamil Sharif and Mick Mullins: aka The Levee Horns.

It's quite an all-star brass section, incidentally. Mullins has backed The Rolling Stones and Bruce Springsteen, while Sharif is a legendary New Orleans musician. Additional vocals come from actor Will Wheaton, no less. The result is a bouncy floor filler with a terrific chorus. I've always loved songs with 'Ay-ay-ay-ay' in them. Check out The Pistols's gnarly version of '(I'm Not Your) Steppin' Stone'.

The location is the beautiful Hollywood hills. The lyric subject is an allegory of infatuation with a girl, symbolising that of a junkie with his addiction. Either way, the protagonist ends up alone: 'And I say/Nobody knows me, I'm all alone/ Ah Ay-ay-ay-ai-ai gotta go'.

'Who Would've Thought' (Armstrong)
This was the third single lifted from *Life*. It has radio-friendly pop melodies with a punk heart, and sing-along chorus that's easy to pick up. The craft shown in this fourth radically different cut halfway through the album, is quite staggering. Vic Ruggiero is prominent, on piano and guitar. It's perfectly arranged; concise, with zero fat.

Tim's lyric is sentimental: something of which he's very capable. It's never been confirmed whom the words relate to, but Brody Dalle is an obvious choice. I think some of the sentiment could be about Tim's friendship with Matt, but it's mainly about Brody, I think. Tim's post-Operation Ivy experience is referenced in the verse:

So, I drank like a fish and crawled like a rat
Through the city of shit, I ended up on my back

The references to Los Angeles' Echo Park, do back up the Brody theory. They lived together in L.A.:

But I can't believe you're with me after dark
So let it come together in Echo Park

It also talks of Tim's lonely feelings when he first arrived in the City of Angels:

And it hits me when I'm alone, I'm an angry man
I start singing to myself, I got dealt a shitty hand

All in all, it's quite autobiographical and sweet. But the melody is killer and was accompanied by a feel-good video featuring lots of sun and Tim on a roof.

'Cash, Culture and Violence' (Armstrong)
This highly individual and unique track is lightning-quick on its feet. The Mighty Bosstones' Dicky Barrett helps out in the chorus. The echo on Tim's voice in the verse, adds to the ram-raid feel, with a melodic 1960s-ish guitar

line working well with his part-sung/part-rapped vocal. Matt's bass line is awesome: phat in tone and groove. The chorus swoops in, and the whole feel is of being aboard a getaway car. All in a predominantly-two-chord structure of F and Bb.

The lyric's theme is the gangster style of society, bureaucracy and authority: legal or otherwise. We live in a world dominated by the sword, the jewel and the imagination. It's a world governed by bullies, money and materialism. It's up to the people to work out where they fit in and what they can do about it; to recognise how things tick. Authorities are no better than the backstreet gangsters at controlling things.

Check out the track's bass-drop mix: mentioned later in the stand-alone singles section.

'Cocktails' (Armstrong)

Fantastic harmonica by Santo Faxio creates a dirty punk-blues vibe. Vic Ruggiero is also there on piano, again. It's another radio-friendly track; Tim again showing his versatility as a vocalist. Of course, the characteristic grit is always there, but this cut's emotion and dexterity are special – especially on the chorus, which has a nice swoop taking the song to a new level.

New York City is the lyric's location, with references to the Lower East Side, Avenue C and Tompkins Square: a park in Manhattan, notorious as a meeting place for drug pushers and users. The central character's squat is on Avenue C. Her drug cocktails were mixed there. The girl in the lyric just wants to know who she's dealing with. No complications or expectations, just honesty please. Not too much to ask for, is it?

'The Wolf' (Armstrong)

This is a biting number; quite old-school with its boogie-style guitar riff filthily distorted to the max. This guitar is the song's engine. It's steady in tempo and crunching in delivery. And the killer chorus is a real lung buster, to be sung with full force. Ollie Lettgenau helps on vocals. 'And I didn't trust him, because he smiled at me first/ Just like The Wolf before he'd bite me'. It's a definite swipe at greedy record-company bosses, and a continuation of the sentiment of 'Disorder and Disarray' on *Wolves*. The original demo features a Jerry Lee Lewis-style hammered piano, which is fantastic, but ultimately didn't make it to the album version.

'1998' (Armstrong, Pyro)

A rare moment on *Life*: two punk tracks sequenced back-to-back. The riff and rhythm of '1998' are deliberately reminiscent of The Clash's '1977'. It has a chord-based hook and a rock-solid backbeat.

The second guitar's discordant melody gives the track a slightly left-field sonic, a bit like 'Black Lung'. The subject matter is not Sid Vicious or nouveau punk, despite the lyric's constant Sid references. Tim co-wrote the song with

Right: Classic MTV era Rancid, four distinct individuals, one unified gang.

Left: Photograph taken by Kathy Bauer. One punk, one skater-kid, one muso and Gilman Street sign.

Right: The band in a video promo from 2014 showcasing three new tracks which soon appeared on *Honor.*

Left: The Debut EP released on Lookout in 1992. Everything you'd want from a young punk band's first release, including its sleeve. (*Lookout*)

Right: The debut LP cover. Note the logo, used on this release and then discarded until it reappeared on 2017's *Trouble Maker*. (*Epitaph*)

Right: The band's second EP. Lars's debut recording, and his impact (left) on the sleeve photograph alone, is stunning. (*Fat Wreck Chords*)

Left: The *Let's Go* front cover. There's a map of the Bay Area, and a determined fist on the right - a call to arms. (*Epitaph*)

Left: The iconic cover to *Wolve* with Lars, photographed by Jesse Fischer. The image is up there with punk's greatest. (*Epitaph*)

Right: 'Time Bomb' 7" Cadillac cover. It propelled Rancid into the mainstream and was voted among NME's top songs of 1995. (*Epitaph*)

Left: 'Took the 60 bus out of downtown Campbell/Ben Zanatto he was on there he was waiting for me.'

Right: The *Life* sleeve. A change from the black and white Zerox-style covers utilised thus far. With classic Rancid ingredients, mind. (*Epitaph*)

Left: A swift return to punk stylings for the fifth album. Note the influence of anarcho-band Crass on its edging. (*Hellcat*)

Right: *Bloodclot* 7" cover. Rehearsal space, tangled wires, Ramones and Dropkick Murphy's posters and Anti Nowhere League daubed on the wall. (*Hellcat*)

Left: Video still from the classic 'Salvation' promo. It was Rancid's breakthrough, especially on MTV where the video seemed to be on repeat in 1994.

Right: Another still from the 'Salvation' video.

Left: Taken from the 1995 'Ruby Soho' video, Tim in the hallway bringing the lyrics to life. It was the 3rd single from *Wolves*.

Right: Another still from the 'Ruby Soho' video with Tim on the periphery, again bringing the lyrical sentiment to life.

Left: A still from the 'Time Bomb' video. A gritty video accompanying the grittiest of ska punk anthems.

Right: Another still from 'Time Bomb'.

Left: A still from 'Hooligans'. The black and white newspaper halftone effect of the video complements the lively 2 Tone style of the song perfectly.

Right: The 2 Tone influence of 'Hooligans' was extended with Roddy Byers, Neville Staples and Lynval Goulding appearing on the recording.

Left: The dreamy pop tones of 'Who Would've Thought' were apparent in its bright video, with sunshine and a blue backdrop.

Right: … though Tim doesn't always look so comfortable in such an environment…

Left: The 'Bloodclot' promo is complete with frayed images and fantastic footage of the band performing the verses.

Right: 'Another 'Bloodclot' still. Punk with a late 1990s glossy edge in its video.

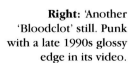

Left: *Indestructible* cover. Different colour scheme, but a classic sleeve nonetheless. (*Hellcat*)

Right: A poster tucked away inside the *Dominoes* sleeve. The image is the same as on the album's front cover. (*Hellcat*)

Right: The *Honor* front cover. SG, Gretsch and P-bass. There's a nice change in colour scheme, too. (*Hellcat*)

Left: The *Trouble Maker* sleeve. Happy with the red and black colour scheme, Rancid also re-used the logo from the band's debut. (*Hellcat*)

Left: The first in a series of stills from the black and white promotional video showcasing new material in 2014. Note Tim's spiderweb head tattoo!

Right: Close up of Matt Freeman at the same sessions. The tracks included were 'Collision Course', 'Honor Is All We Know' and 'Evil's My Friend'.

Left: Lars now adopting a skinhead-style get-up in 2014.

Right: All round one mic.

Left: Branden Steineckert slotted right into the brotherhood of Rancid, his powerhouse drumming pushing the band on to new levels.

Right: These tracks, of course, appeared on 2014's *Honor*.

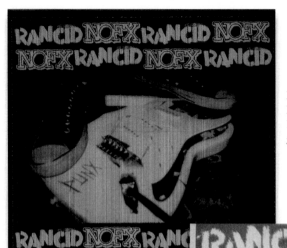

Left: Sleeve from the NOFX/ Rancid split album released on BYO in 2002. Also available in green. (*BYO*)

Right: The 'Hooligans' 7" front cover. (*Hellcat*)

Left: The 'Sick Sick World' 12" single cover. The release was interesting as the title track was actually on the B-side. (*Hellcat*)

Right: The front cover of the 2016 compilation *All The Moon Stompers*. Spot the individual characters and what they're holding! (*Randale*)

Left: Split 7" front/back (you decide) cover with Cock Sparrer. Cock Sparrer's anthem of belonging was rerecorded for this release. (*Pirates Press*)

Right: Split 7" front/back cover. Singles were initially available at joint shows celebrating Sparrer's 40th, and Rancid's 20th anniversaries. (*Pirates Press*)

Left: Early 'All Age' gig poster for 924 Gilman Street. No drugs, no alcohol.

Below: More posters, actually included in the artwork of *Let's Go*. Lots of legendary names, some famous, most not.

Left: Say no more.

Howie Pyro from D Generation. Howie was a friend of Sid's and was reportedly one of the last people to see him alive, having been with Sid on the night of his fatal heroin overdose. It's about Howie and his punk-rock life. Things don't change, and 'Hanging out with Sid' is a metaphor for the lifestyle's continuity: 'Hanging out with Sid yet again in the USA'.

'1998' is a timeline of Howie, kids and punk from the 1970s to 1998. The Sidney chorus might grab the listener, but the lyric focuses on old and new punks equally.

'Lady Liberty' (Armstrong)

This is rockabilly, reproduced faithfully with Brett's brilliant, snapping, clicking drum pattern. The rhythm never drops for a second, and the track is one the album's highlights. The guitar work – clear as a bell and twice as spunky – is slick, rapid, and executed with panache by both players. Lars sings 'Lady Liberty' brilliantly, and it's the band's most authentic rockabilly song to date. It marks a series of such numbers spread across the midsection of the band's career.

The words could've been by Joe Strummer for sure – a return to politics, and a swipe at the hypocrisy of the United States, which promises, for instance, free speech, and then shuts people up for doing too much of it.

> Lady Liberty, come down and bleed to me
> I want nothing to do with your crazy world
> Broken promises, those poor noises

The world politics references are most interesting – examples of the US meddling on the world stage, in Afghanistan, with the Kremlin, and in South America (Nicaragua): 'From the Contras, to the upstarts who shouted 'Sandinista''. The Sandinistas were Nicaragua rebels who overthrew the Somoza dictatorship in 1979. Their attempts to form a government were ultimately thwarted by the Contra War of 1979-1981, with the USA backing the Contras: opponents of the Sandinistas. Free speech and liberty indeed, eh? The track is a great example of Rancid addressing a serious international subject in the guise of a rockin' number. And of course, it was the title of The Clash's fourth and coincidentally most-experimental album.

'Wrongful Suspicion' (Armstrong, Vic Ruggiero)

Lars treats us to a roll call of Rancid's favourite Big Apple artists, before inviting Tim to step in with the opening verse on this blues number. One of these artists – David Hillyard – appears again as part of the brass section with Mark Mullins and Jamil Sharif: a legendary trio whose presence no doubt shaped the track's Bourbon Street sonic.

Tim's voice works well surrounded by all this. The gutsy, soulful vocal delivers an account of unfair police attention, and ultimately, brutality. It's kind

of like a civil-rights protest song: a typical theme for blues songs from the likes
of Robert Johnson. Co-writer Vic Ruggiero from The Slackers plays piano on
the track.

Of course, many of the acts in the roll call (by now Rancid's mates) would
end up releasing material on Hellcat: the label Tim set up with Brett Gurewitz.
Indeed, *Life* would be Rancid's final release on Epitaph.

'Turntable' (Armstrong)
This has a real Wurlitzer vibe, and is foot-to-the-floor and loaded with tasty,
raunchy guitar licks like the one at the end of the first chorus. Indeed, guest
guitarist Simon Chardiet was utilised. It's an example of the quality Rancid
deep cuts.

The variety of music Tim penned for *Life* was a definite taste of things
to come, showing the breadth of his songwriting. The subject matter of
'Turntable' is real life and how quickly it can change, together with a message
of unity. Life is over before you know it, so don't spend time hating and
creating divisions. Unite; live together as one. You can be up one minute, down
the next: 'Come on everybody let's get together/I appall the backdrop of hate'.

'Something In The World Today' (Armstrong, Frederiksen)
A punk rock balancer, with Lars back centre-stage as vocalist (helped by
Agnostic Front's Roger Miret) and writer. This is one of the album's five songs
he wrote with Tim. There were no songs written by Matt and Tim, and for the
second consecutive album, no lead vocals from Matt. Indeed, he wasn't even
credited with any backing vocals.

The guitar riff in D has a melodic suspended-4th slant to it: very street-punk.
When the second guitar joins in thrashing out the chords, it is powerful.
It's high tempo, though not high-octane. Lars's voice is – as ever – strong,
masculine and full of character. It's an urgent-sounding, edgy shot of punk,
with plenty of lyric hints at punk rock's history, like 'Babylon's burning' (The
Ruts) and the 'come right back for you' lyric which nods at Sham 69's 'Borstal
Breakout': 'Oh oh oh oh oh nine lives/I'm gonna come right back for you'.
Rancid's appreciation of what went before, is one of their most appealing
qualities – whether it be lyrical, covering classic tunes, or releasing new
material on Hellcat by the likes of Joe Strummer or GBH. Combine this with
their obvious support for their peers ('Wrongful Suspicion'), and you see a
band fully immersed in the punk network and giving it plenty back.

'Corazon De Oro' (Armstrong)
This title is Spanish for 'Heart of gold', in case you didn't know. It's the album's
second love song that Tim wrote for Brody Dalle – or rather, it's a love song
for Tim's ideal girlfriend? I'm not saying, incidentally, that Brody was or wasn't!
The sentimental, heartfelt lyrics have a slight hint of desperation – desperation
for anyone who travels, therefore being away from someone you love. It can be

a dark place: with your mind on the girl and what she may be doing. It doesn't necessarily help one's mental well-being.

> And I got nothing but abandonment
> Nothing but a silhouette girl
> Into the darkness I sing

Of course, Brody Dalle was making her way with The Distillers, so this rock-'n'-roll marriage was a two-way street. Tim was looking for his *corazon de oro*.

The track has a dreamy tone, a clear arrangement, and is gorgeously poppy. Oh, and Will Wheaton helps on vocals.

'Coppers' (Armstrong, Frederiksen, Dr. Israel)

Life closes with one of its most diverse tracks: especially for a punk band. Caribbean folk music – notably Trinidadian calypso and Jamaican mento – are in the mix on 'Coppers'. Steve Perkins plays steel drums throughout, and the tempo is a steady, not-quite modern reggae rhythm, but something more traditional and rural sounding. Obviously, the offbeat emphasis, remains.

This was co-written with Dr. Israel aka Douglas Bennett, who released a healthy catalogue of material from the late-1990s onwards, which included a dub-mix 45 of 'Coppers' with the band: credited to Rancid vs Dr. Israel. Bennett toasts and ad-libs superbly on the album version, working in conjunction with Tim and Lars' lead vocals. The result has a disparate beauty.

The lyric takes us to some of the locations and – at times – studios where *Life* was recorded. Obviously, this gives the track an exotic feel. New York City, Coyote Studios, Brixton, Kingston, Waterhouse and Los Angeles. The theme focuses on street violence and struggles, gangs and brutality across the world, with the inevitable call for unity and humility, rather than mere sympathy and a resignation to the continuation of things as they are. If we become one, there's nothing to fight about, right? Idealistic maybe, but life won't wait, eh?

> 'Come' I said, 'Put down your rachet now
> Rude boy, set down your gun
> L.A., Kingston, New York and London
> Move, nobody fight form together as one
> This gun pressure soon be over and done

Contemporary Releases
'Hooligans'/'Cash, Culture And Violence'(Bass Drop Mix)/'Things To Come' (Dance Hall Mix) (7", CD single)

Release date: UK: 1998, Chart Position: UK: 162
Not released in the US, where only a promo CD was issued.

A-side
'Hooligans' (Armstrong, Frederiksen, Vic Ruggiero)
The *Life Won't Wait* version.

'Cash, Culture And Violence' (Bass Drop Mix) (Armstrong)
This is astonishing. It is an entirely different recording to the breakneck-speed track that appeared on *Life*. Arguably it's the single-most-experimental thing Rancid have ever done. With its dirty harmonica, sassy horns, and bhangra-style drumming, it's almost unrecognisable as Rancid, until the vocals hit. Some have even referred to it as one of the first dubstep recordings. It's a marriage of Eastern rhythms with Western music.

B-side
'Things To Come' (Armstrong)
This is a wonderfully soulful song, with a political thrust to the lyric. The dance hall reference is more to actual old-school dance halls. It has warm horn work, a simple steady rhythm, and a swoony vibe, rather than the hedonistic, digital riddim-based dancehall reggae-influenced by Jamaican dancehall musician Wayne Smith's 'Under Mi Sleng Teng'.

'Things To Come' appeared on the expanded edition of *Life,* and on several official band compilations which will be covered later.

'Hooligans' (Armstrong, Frederiksen, Vic Ruggiero)
Release date: 1998, Chart position: Did not chart
The same version as the album. Released in the US and Japan as a promo.

'Bloodclot'/'Endrina'/'Stop' (7", CD single)
Release date: 1998, Chart positions: UK: 83, US: Did not chart
This sleeve is cool, showing the band's rehearsal space. The picture is given a bright aerosol spray job, and features posters of Anti-Nowhere League and Ramones, among others.

A-side
'Bloodclot' (Armstrong, Frederiksen)
The same version as on the album.

B-side
'Endrina' (Armstrong)
The riff is reminiscent of both The Jam's 'In the City' and Sex Pistols' 'Holidays In The Sun': a good starting point. 'Endrina' is a great song, aggressive at crucial moments, with an attacking, raw guitar solo. Brett's drum rolls are great in the build to the guitar solo, signalled by Tim's cry of 'Endrina!'. The guitar-

playing throughout is raw and riffy: quite Paul Weller-esque. Matt drives out an incredibly busy bass line. It really is a track best heard on its 7" vinyl issue, which allows resonance and energy to fizz out of the speakers. This was the opening track on the Hellcat compilation *Give 'Em The Boot 6*.

'Stop' (Armstrong)

A cracking slice of understated ska from the boys. Warm brass, lively kick, and delicious rolling bass from Matt. The backing vocals are very effective and soulful, and the cut shows why Rancid were getting such a good reputation for crafting songs at this point.

Tim's lyric focusses on positivity. No matter what the detractors say about your life and attitude, it's up to you to either lie back and take it, or fight on through it all and come out on top. 'Stop' was included on the 2015 compilation *All the Moon Stompers.*

'Bloodclot' (Armstrong, Frederiksen)

Release date: 1998, Chart position: Did not chart

A promo CD single issued to US radio. This was a censored version, minus the expletives in the second verse. A limited run of just 500 vinyl copies was also issued.

'Who Would've Thought' (Armstrong)

Release date: 1998, Chart position: Did not chart

A CD promo issued in the US. This is the album version.

Life Won't Wait (Expended edition) (2017)

An expanded edition of *Life* with 'Things To Come' included as a bonus.

Rancid (LP) (2000)

Personnel:
Tim Armstrong, Lars Frederiksen: guitars, vocals
Matt Freeman: bass, vocals
Brett Reed: drums
Label: Hellcat
Producer: Brett Gurewitz
Release date: 1 August 2000
Chart positions: US: 68, UK: 68
Running time: 38:31

Rancid were always a band second, and mates first. Tim and Matt had known each other since they were five years old. They became close friends as they both got into punk and were joined by Brett and Lars, both from the punk network. So, with the experimentation on *Wolves* and especially *Life*, the band found themselves risking being alienated by parts of the punk network: the more narrow-minded bit. Despite the spirit of punk being about the liberty to do what you want to do and not what's expected of you, experimentation doesn't necessarily wash with every self-righteous member of the punk world.

After extensively touring in 1998/1999, the question again was where Rancid would go next? The answer turned out to be very simple – rather than go out even further afield up any remaining unexplored backstreets, they made it clear their next album would be a punk one. Nothing else. Punk fuckin' rock. Tim said so in interviews. The result was *Rancid*. Yes, another eponymous release, following the debut EP and LP. It will be referred to here as *Rancid 5*, though some call it *Rancid 2000*. It's one of their best-loved albums. Everything about it is punk rock – power chords reign; the hard-as-hell sound. It's brutal at times. The 22 tracks clock in at less than 40 minutes. Matt sings some lead vocals for the first time since *Let's Go*.

The cover was Xerox-style black and white: very do-it-yourself; Crass-esque. This was the brainchild of Kristen Vanderlip, Lars and Tim. Its raw appeal spoke volumes to die-hard punks, with its back patch and t-shirt potential. It looked threatening, with guerrilla-warfare character.

Rancid 5 was released in do-it-yourself style on Tim Armstrong's new record label Hellcat, which surfaced in 1997. It was a joint venture between Brett Gurewitz and Tim, under the Epitaph wing. Tim was at the creative hub of an exciting era in American underground music, with a clutch of artists writing strong material, and in Hellcat they found a label very much on the same page, enthusiastically supporting them and punk rock music.

Early Hellcat releases included discs from Dropkick Murphys, The Slackers, F-Minus, The Distillers and Agnostic Front. A series of collections entitled *Give 'Em The Boot* showcased a batch of new Hellcat artists, and were crucial in introducing these esoteric artists to UK audiences. The collections were augmented with familiar names like The Business and were a definite throwback to the early days of punk and new wave compilations. And the fact they were issued regularly, was another plus.

In 2000, Rancid started issuing their own material on Hellcat, and *Rancid 5* was a revelation. The material on the first Rancid LP was angry high-octane punk rock with plenty of hardcore elements. As Matt put it to *Slap* magazine in 2000, 'We were angry'. When *Slap* asked him if the band had intended to make another hardcore punk record in 2000, he replied, 'No, we were just fucking pissed. There was a lot of tension in the world. It was coming from a place of pure anger. We put it down and that was the result'.

The LP had a whiplash quality, up there with anything released on Discord or Revelation Records in the 1980s. However, the album had nuance. Anger was present, but for a different reason. It was more macro-anger at the world around them than at their own situation. The band channelled their travels and experiences. But more importantly, the band's musical evolution had given them that crucial ingredient: craft. And now, that craft was laced into what Rancid did originally.

'Don Giovanni' (Armstrong)
For a brief second, the jangly opening chords sound like Led Zeppelin's 'The Song Remains the Same'. However, any remaining resemblance is soon given the boot. The track then charges into a ferocious assault and is a synopsis of the Mozart opera of the same name. Highbrow, *see*. The sword fight between Giovanni and Anya's father, led to the latter's death. And of course, the character came back from the dead, and took Giovanni to hell. But you know that, *right*. The message is, that you get what you deserve, and this is very definitely an allegory for so many people in the modern world. You reap what you sow. The wonderfully tight and abrupt coda, underlines this: 'So don't fuck with me, kid!'.

The track is just 35 seconds long, with all three vocalists immediately contributing. The simple harmony behind the main hook is an early example of the band's acquired craft. It fires its warning: 'You're making enemies/Like Don Giovanni'.

'Disgruntled' (Armstrong)
This scorcher of a track jumps straight in without any gap after 'Don Giovanni'. You could be forgiven for thinking they were the same track but in two parts. It's Hardcore punk in E major, with aggressive guitars, Matt's million-notes-per-second bass line, and Brett's lightning drumstick work. Tim and Lars vocal interchanges, work like clockwork – their different tonal qualities delivering the enraged lyric with 110 per cent passion and even-more commitment. The target is hit. That target is the behaviour of authorities who use police tactics and power to wipe out freedoms and the tools of freedom: 'Let's go, let's go/ Disgruntled'.

'It's Quite Alright' (Armstrong)

This is the first example of Rancid as craftsmen working brilliantly with the album's hardcore sound. It's one of the band's finest moments. What makes it, is Tim's deliciously laconic vocal. It works seemingly at odds with the backing's speed and power. All words are easily decipherable, and as a result, this is different to the spit and rage on *Rancid*. Tim's voice has true soul. Fusing this with the ferocious backing, sets Rancid apart from so many others. The descending riff in C is a high-speed bulldozer. The guitars slash over a pummelling backbeat.

The theme of the reality of life is at odds with the façade and pretence of the establishment and governments' public-relations version. The reality is your life; your freedom.

> All systems can stop right here
> And all we are is pretend
> Some things can be a mystery
> And all we are is freedom

'Let Me Go' (Armstrong)

Somehow – quite deliberately I'm sure – Rancid seemed to create a new rhythm here. It hints of Op Ivy ska, with a danceable heavy thud. When the intro is done and the groove kicks in, we have a spacey guitar floating over Brett's drum pattern: space-hardcore-ska if you will. Lars and Tim's fretwork is full of finesse – clean tones behind the verse, with wonderful wah-wah and chorus effects flooding the instrumental passages. It creates a soundscape of feeling lost, exploring a new astrological world.

Again, Tim takes the lead vocal. The grit in the man's voice is given room, as the backing isn't always full-on. The crunching chords only really surface in the chorus.

> Correction, I need no direction
> Oh let me go one last time
> I spend my whole life searching for direction
> Oh let me go just one last time
> You can burn a book if you don't like the answers

The lyric focuses on people who need to be led. Some don't necessarily have the faculty to think for themselves – the CNN generation: force-fed information and direction. Or to put it in the modern world: the internet social-media generation. Those who *do* possess the faculty to think for themselves, often find answers they don't like, but at least they're looking.

'I Am Forever' (Armstrong)

It's Lars who leads the hardcore charge on *Rancid 5*. He takes the lead vocal on several short hardcore blasts, roaring out the words. 'I Am Forever' has power chords (B/D/F#), full hardcore rage, superb guitar work, and is done-and-dusted in 64 seconds.

It's a sad lyric, though, about letting people down, and the need to change. Time is all that can ultimately precipitate that change. The protagonist is the only one in their life with the capability to do what they've done. Things will happen around them, but they must live with themselves forever, on Earth and in the afterlife. Therefore, it's up to them to seek redemption, and change before it's too late. 'Doors bust open, doors slam shut/The key to change is time'.

'Poison' (Armstrong)

An underrated classic, brilliant lyrically, with more cultural references. Tim must've been immersing himself in classic works like *Don Giovanni*, and now *The Canterbury Tales* by 14th-century poet Geoffrey Chaucer. *The Canterbury Tales* was designed to entertain a group of pilgrims on a journey. Each verse, often lengthy, was told by a person in a certain position in society – for example, 'The Miller's Tale', 'The Wife Of Bath's Tale' and, in this case, 'The Pardoner's Tale'. The Pardoner used to collect taxes from ordinary folk, in return for saving their soul from hell and damnation, or so he claimed. You see, greed and extortion date back to those times – something that was still alive and kicking in the year 2000. And in 2022, as it goes.

Accusations have been made from the very beginning
Some people are poison
Under my skin like opium

Tim explores all of this against a bulldozing, shuddering hardcore backing with frenetic and unbelievably fast bass-playing by Matt. Guitar chords ring out, allowing Tim to deliver his words easily, emphasised with expletives, viewpoints, suffering and Cold War references. Thus, it's a great marriage of cultural and modern references. Full backing vocals during the chorus, complete the job.

'Loki' (Armstrong)

Another hardcore blast from Lars; no-nonsense punk rock, bellowed out. Loki is of course the original Norse god of destruction and chaos, and is the inspiration for this song. Any insane world leader or authoritarian thinks they are Loki at times. Anger energises their behaviour, and of course, this can end in disaster. What's important are the consequences of the aggression, and often this is bad news, with innocent victims.

With all the guns going off, who can say no to the guy
Who watch out, who's fucking nuts
Cause Loki's playing tricks again

It's another example of the band taking an intellectual theme and turning it into awesome punk rock. But not only that: hardcore punk rock affects lives. With lyrics that are meaningful and spell things out, consequences of violence can be explained, for example. Having such aggressive music creates an outlet for young anger to be channelled. Therefore, many angry young people turn out to be not-so-angry adults. 'In a violent crazy world spewing words of madness/It can go either way, you know'.

'Black Hawk Down' (Armstrong)

A swipe at US foreign policy, the continual interfering in overseas nations, but then leaving the job incomplete. This approach stretches back to Vietnam, more recently Afghanistan and, in this case, Somalia. *Black Hawk Down* was a 1993 Ridley Scott film. The US – with good intention – tried to bring humanitarian aid to those suffering in the domestic conflict, by using Black Hawk helicopters. Somalian forces attacked two of them and, from then on, US soldiers struggled. Those soldiers bore the brunt of US foreign policy and civil hatred.

The title is also a street term: gang terminology for the sound of a shotgun being fired. It's powerhouse, exhilarating punk. Tim sprawls out the words, reminiscent of the band's early work – a nice blast from the past in a way, but it still carries Rancid's lyric evolution.

'Rwanda' (Armstrong)

Global troubles again, where the everyday population suffer, such as the 1994 Rwandan Civil War. The genocide in Rwanda was a heart-breaking episode, with between 500,000 and 1,000,000 people losing their lives at the hands of the armed Militia. The song is a clear tribute to the people of this beautiful African country, and sends out support.

Rwanda, yeah your moon shines bright
Rwanda, over planned genocide
Rwanda, won't you be strong like a lion

It's a huge chorus – a lung buster, inviting audiences to shout these words as loud as they can. Music can unite, its call going across continents. The song didn't change the course of events, but it has heart and feeling, and it would be nice to know whether it reached anyone who survived or who descended from these times. Rancid – attempting to spread unity across the miles.

The tempo is slower, and the song more-melodic – one of two of the album's tracks that deviate from the brutal hardcore sound but are still punk rock.

'Corruption' (Armstrong, Frederiksen, Freeman)

The welcome return of Matt Freeman as lead vocalist. It's shared with Lars, but still, Matt's distinctive cookie-monster growl is back on 'Corruption', loved by all members of the Rancid nation.

The song is ferocious, hardcore all the way, and every bit as angry as the title suggests. It's a tirade against governments and religion, and the consequences of their actions are made clear. The use of religious symbolism enhances the sarcastic lyric, as if poking fun at the evangelists and priests who threaten the rest of us if we don't get down on our knees and fucking-well pray.

At 2:08 in length, it's one of the album's longer numbers.

'Antennas' (Armstrong)

Another clever, sophisticated piece of songwriting from Tim. The arrangement is superb, crafted with light and shade, with room for Tim's laconic snarl to perform fully. 'Antennas' is a masterpiece, the lyrics biting, hitting out with venom at those who exploit California. Tim's talking about Hollywood executives, record company sharks and business people squeezing every buck they can from the state. These folk send out their feelers and scouts to look for opportunities and rinse them to the max. These feelers and scouts (the antennas) are as much a part of the problem as are their employers.

Your antennas are pointed in the right direction
You make a deal with any situation
So, with no evacuation
Let California fall into the fucking ocean

The whole thing is played with dexterity and power where needed, and an eerie quiet when words need emphasizing. And remember, Epic Records sent out their own antennas to Rancid, as did Madonna.

'Rattlesnake' (Armstrong)

Speaking of phoneys, music bandwagons have a lot to answer for. The history of contemporary music has been littered with acts that adopt an image or a genre. Fake punk rockers especially. This is about people who say they are punk when they ain't. You can take your pick who this is aimed at, but some are more obvious than others, right?

Fuck That Shit, I don't want to hear it
You can't bare it when we blare it
I hate your band, you understand
You got no passion, it's all fashion

Phoneys and fakes aren't just restricted to bands of course. Gilman Street was invaded by record company sharks in the early-1990s after Green Day became massive. Rancid had already written many a song about this ('Disorder and Disarray'), and had their own experience with it, as chronicled in 'The 11th Hour'. 'Rattlesnake' continues the theme.

75

A mention must be given to the huge, metallic guitar riffage on this cut. This opens the track and subsequently drops in and out.

One final postscript – it's been rumoured that 'Rattlesnake' was written in response to a song by The Queers titled 'Rancid Motherfucker'. Joe Queer was mates with Rancid, and reportedly The Queers' song was written in response to something he heard a Rancid-t-shirt-wearing fan scream at a show by The Vandals. 'Play something good you rancid motherfucker', the fan allegedly bellowed. I have no idea if this really happened, as I wasn't present, but who knows, eh?

'Not To Regret' (Armstrong)
One of the ultimate overlooked Rancid cuts, in my view. The gutsy, bluesy guitar work merges brilliantly with the hardcore juggernaut backing. And when Tim's raw-as-fuck gritty, soulful delivery is thrown in on top, we have perfection. Look at the biblical references crossing over with the apparent sinful activities:

> Someone shout out hallelujah,
> Roulette spinner blackjack winner
> Everybody tells me to look within
> But I'll look within the city of sin

Gospel swamp hardcore punk rock, anyone? The dichotomy of sin city and the word of God, justifying the art of the gambler and the choice they make.

'Radio Havana' (Armstrong)
The pace slows and the melodies rise for the second time, with the catchiest of choruses. The result is another huge track that could've easily been on *Wolves*. It was issued to radio stations and DJs as a promo single in the US. I know a few Rancid fans who dislike this one. I'm not sure why, but possibly its presence on the band's most hardcore album, is why. It is different to a lot of the other brutal, frenetic cuts. These same folk say the same about 'Rwanda'. Personally, I like balance on an LP, and the fact that the other twenty cuts are fast and hardcore is enough for me.

Recordings of radio commentary are used, which adds to the quality of the track. It begins with a quirky piece of guitar, and its root-note musical chassis encourages the natural melody. There are great backing vocals in the breakdown sections. In all, the song is superbly arranged and crafted.

Obviously, it's about Cuba: only before the Castro revolution. Before Castro came to power in 1959, Cuba – and Havana in particular – was a tourist and nightlife hot spot, rife with the most exciting and alluring nightclubs and cabaret shows. With Castro in power, austerity, poverty and a puritan way of life became the norm. The glitz and glamour were replaced by run-down buildings and government-run radio and music services. Liberal thinking and art were no longer encouraged, and there could be consequences for anyone dumb enough to try it, as Joe Strummer put it. Thus, the cars and music you see on the streets were pre-Castro, like Cuba and Havana had become frozen in time. Everything you saw and heard were from the 1950s: Cadillacs, for instance.

'It's a fugitive of time/Radio Havana'. The chorus is apt. Havana is a fugitive of time indeed. It's a very sad lyric. But some of the best music in the world has meaningful, melancholy words. To marry these words with a sweet melody as roots reggae does, or with uplifting, fist-pumping sounds as Rancid do, is the nirvana.

'Axiom' (Armstrong, Frederiksen, Freeman)

This one is kind of in two halves. Top-speed hardcore velocity is constant. However, the first half is all about Matt Freeman and his out-of-this-world bass solo. How the man can play a Fender Precision bass so fast while retaining resonance and the instrument's natural frequency, is incredible.

Howling siren guitars, colour the track elsewhere. Not to be outdone, Lars delivers an incredible vocal performance in the second half. The man could fill an entire stadium with his roar, without the need for a PA, I'm sure. It's a nasty-sounding thing, 'Axiom', and is about sticking up for yourself on the street: urban blight once more.

'Black Derby Jacket' (Armstrong)

A hardcore ballad really, over a surfabilly backbeat. Tim's words are sung entirely by Matt. At long last – after waiting for two entire albums – we get him back in front of the mic. It's a heart-warming lyric about Tim and Matt's relationship in those early days around Gilman Street.

> You left in a plane, I left in a van
> Played nightclubs, house parties, and auditoriums
> Saw Germany, England, Italy with my band
> I know you better than your new friends

That last line is profound. It's a statement of the depth of their relationship. Remember, back in those times, Matt grudgingly got on with his life while Tim struggled with alcoholism and drug dealers. The lyric moves through those years, and the chorus repetitions – particularly when Matt sings the final chorus: slowed down with just his bass – are beautifully tender.

> But I got a perspective on you
> All the good and bad that we went through
> I know you better than you know you
> Cause I've got a new perspective on you

Tim recorded the song under his Tim Timebomb moniker in April 2013, and it was covered by Left Alone in 2015.

'Meteor Of War' (Armstrong)

The first of two back-to-back bullet tracks shows a definite early-1980s UK hardcore influence. Rancid are punk rock fans, historians, and by now, heroes. The way they honour stalwarts such as Discharge, The Exploited and GBH, has always been endearing to me. GBH supported Rancid on tour in the early-2000s.

'Meteors Of War' sees Tim taking the lead vocal, and his throat-full-of-razor-blades style has more than a passing resemblance to The Exploited singer Wattie. It's an all-action number, primarily using muted C and F chords in the verse, fast as you like. The repeated 'John Brown' chants were made for a live performance, inviting call-and-response from the crowd. John Brown was a 19th-century American abolitionist. He famously led a raid on a weapons store at Harper's Ferry, Virginia. He also tried to lead a slavery rebellion prior to the Civil War, and was arrested and subsequently executed.

'Dead Bodies' (Armstrong, Frederiksen)

The second UKHC cut. Lars leads the charge here on another spectacular raid of hard-hitting punk rock. And this, arguably, is Rancid's hardest song. The chorus is so reminiscent of Stoke-on-Trent's finest: Discharge. Lars' voice lends itself to this kind of work, its pile-driving quality giving as much as it gets from the backing track. The lyrics are brutal.

> Dead Bodies everywhere
> Piles of blood and entrails and hair
> I'm bleeding from the Armageddon outside

The theme is the brutality of war and violence: an obvious choice for such a hard number. Given the breadth of intellect and subject matter on what's basically a hardcore punk LP, we can forgive Rancid for plumping for the obvious here.

Nekromantix covered this song superbly on their self-titled 2005 album.

'Rigged On A Fix' (Armstrong)

The race for the finish line intensifies with this Matt Freeman-sung speedster. Barely a breath is taken after the previous two tracks.

It's another interesting theme: TV and media generally brainwash a nation and its population. This was never more evident than when the TV quiz show *Twenty-One* let a game show contestant (Charles Van Doren) cheat and win, in order for the show to improve ratings. This was not only immortalised in this track, but in the film *Quiz Show*. It doesn't just tell the story of Van Doren but uses him as a metaphor for society being dulled into accepting whatever the media tells it.

'Young Al Capone' (Armstrong, Frederiksen)

Like on *Life*, this psychobilly number almost steals the show, but this time it's even more at lightning speed, with everything louder, faster and bigger. The opening rock-'n'-roll guitar riff provides the start gun. The guitar licks – nifty and high in the mix – shine through over another mesmerising bass line. The snappy, sharp rhythm drives the track. This is my favourite track on the record. Like 'Lady liberty' on *Life*, 'Young Al Capone' is about a hero sticking up for the working class: 'In the army of Babylon, I'm a young Al Capone/Myself an outlaw in the eyes of the Lord'. He takes things into his own hands. The working class are the army of Babylon, with the reality of their position on the factory floor not at all sugarcoated: 'The third world working on the factory floor/It's so dark in there you can't see the sun no more'. The biblical and gangster references once again lift the lyric content.

The switch in style on this number – like 'Rwanda', 'Radio Havana' and even 'Black Derby Jacket' – gives the album, balance. A great vocal by Lars: needless to say.

'Reconciliation' (Armstrong)
The sprint to the line intensifies with Matt taking the lead baton once more on this chunk of hardcore. It questions regimes. Why when the individuals in power surely know what's right on a humane level – do countries end up divided? Rich and poor; black and white. The focus here is on South Africa and Apartheid: 'Nelson spent 19 years on Robben Island, estranged'. Hardcore stuff, over a C/F power-chord barrage.

'Golden Gate Fields' (Armstrong)
A wonderful song. Tim takes the lead vocal, and as ever, it's full of rasp and grit. There's also a shedload of soul. His delivery is on the laconic side, but this lets him articulate the theme of never losing track of where you come from.

The lyric's location is Tim's young life in Berkeley: in particular, the racetrack not far from where he lived. Golden Gate Fields is in Albany, California, and for years has hosted sports, including horse racing. The character list includes the old men of El Cerrito – who chew the fat over their picks – a jockey Pincay and a horse called Big L. The metaphor here is not *backing the winner* but backing the horse with the biggest heart: that one, ultimately, will get you the farthest.

The location is switched away from the racetrack, to the street. I love the detail about a vision Tim had – when a young buddy of his rode up to the young Tim on his little sister's pink 10-speed pink bike. The hypothetical question is asked: 'Hey Tim, Tim, don't you remember me?/Back in 1973/ And then he was gone, like a flash'. I love this kind of sentiment. It's something often overlooked amidst the working-class fight, urban blight and political comment in Tim's lyrics. The song is evocative of the Great American Songbook. The backing is almost secondary: its sole job to support the words. 'Golden Gate Fields' was also included on *Give 'Em The Boot Volume 3*.

And so, the album draws to its conclusion. In my view, *Rancid 5* was probably the band's finest hour. True, it didn't shift the units of its two immediate predecessors, but by taking themselves back to the very core of their being, and adding what they'd learnt, Rancid had indeed backed the horse with the biggest heart. The race winner shifted more units, but the horse with the heart had the biggest impact. By far.

Contemporary Releases
'Let Me Go'/'Ben Zanotto'/'Dead And Gone' (7" single)
UK Release Date: 16 October 2000. Chart position: UK: 188
This was released on Hellcat Records in the UK and the Netherlands, and on Epitaph in Japan. It was not released in the US. The sleeve was very do-it-yourself, again with a Crass Xerox look, despite the front cover's slightly space-age-looking skull. The 7" picture disc featured a pistol across the middle.

A-side
'Let Me Go' (Armstrong)
Same version as on the album.

B-side
'Ben Zanotto' (Armstrong, Frederiksen)
Ben Zanotto was a friend of Lars, and part of the Skunx gang of punks in Campbell, California. He was immortalised not only in this song, but in the opening lyric to 'Roots Radicals'. The gang themselves were the subject of Lars' song 'Skunx' from Lars Frederiksen and the Bastards' debut LP. It's a heartfelt tribute to someone Lars used to meet up with and hang out with and go to shows with in his young punk days. Their friendship remained until Ben's untimely demise in 1999 from an overdose.

'Dead And Gone' (Armstrong, Frederiksen)
Matt takes the lead vocal. The track is blisteringly quick, pausing to catch its breath midway before setting off again at breakneck speed. The guitar-playing is riff based, repeated hypnotically as the track progresses, creating a crescendo.

'Let Me Go' (CD, Promo)
Release Date: 2000, Chart position: Did not chart
CD promo single to US radio.

'Radio Havana' (CD single, Promo)
Release date: 2000, Chart position: Did not chart
Released to US radio only, this is a different mix, unavailable anywhere else. It was mixed by Los Angeles producer Jack Plug, who has worked with No Doubt, The Black Crowes and Green Day. And very cool it is too.

Rancid 5 (Expanded edition) (2017)

A deluxe version of *Rancid 5* was issued in 2017, with the stand-alone 12"
single 'Sick Sick World' included as a bonus cut. Information on the track can
be found later in the book.

Indestructible (LP) (2003)

Personnel:
Tim Armstrong, Lars Frederiksen: guitar, vocals
Matt Freeman: bass, vocals
Brett Reed: drums
Label: Hellcat
Producer: Brett Gurewitz
Release date: 19 August 2003
Chart positions: US: 15, UK: 29
Running time: 53:07

A lot happened between the releases of *Rancid 5* and *Indestructible*.
Obviously, there was 9/11; Tim Armstrong and Brody Dalle got divorced in
2003; Lars Frederiksen's brother Rob Dapello died in 2001, and Joe Strummer
– inspiration of a generation – died in 2002.

Tim and Brody had married in 1997 when Brody was 18. Tim had just turned
30 at the time. His joy at the union was articulated on two *Life* tracks. The
Distillers – Brody's three-piece all-action punk outfit – were signed to Hellcat,
and it cannot be doubted that Tim helped create a decent platform for the
band. That said, their eponymous debut and *Sing Sing Death House* are terrific.
As is *Coral Fang*.

But by 2003, the relationship was floundering, and this was exacerbated
when Tim saw a picture of Brody with Queens Of The Stone Age's Josh
Homme in *Rolling Stone* magazine. Brody and Tim split soon after, Brody
accusing him of controlling her. Tim's camp were also accused of blocking
The Distillers. A bitter divorce followed. Tim was devastated. Life's tapestry,
eh?

Lars' brother Robert (Rockin' Rob) Dapello had introduced the young Lars
to punk rock music and culture. He was one of the Skunx in Campbell. Shortly
after watching a band in San Jose one Saturday night in February 2001, Rob
complained of feeling ill. He suffered a brain aneurysm and tragically passed
away later that evening.

When Joe Strummer passed away in December 2002, many people's
lives – including mine – would never be the same. By then I had my own
underground live venue and club The Attik, in Leicester, England. It had
an underground clientele with punk spirit at its heart. I wouldn't have had
the inspiration to do this without Joe Strummer's positivity, and I wanted
to harness some of his determination. In the aftermath of Joe's passing, the
atmosphere in The Attik was surreal. It was like he was still with us; like his
soul lived on in us. We couldn't believe he was gone. Joe's albums with The
Mescaleros – *Rock Art And The X-Ray Style*, *Global A Go-Go* and *Streetcore* –
were released on Hellcat. Listening to 'Coma Girl' – the opening cut on the
posthumous *Streetcore* – still brings a lump to my throat. I bet Tim, Lars, Matt
and Brett experienced a similar emotion.

Away from such sadness and tragedy, Rancid immersed themselves in a series of side projects. Lars formed Lars Frederiksen and the Bastards, releasing an eponymous debut album on Hellcat in 2001. It was a punchy collection of punk tunes, including the cover of the aforementioned 'To Have and To Have Not'.

Tim put together the supergroup Transplants with Matt, and Travis Barker of Blink-182. Their self-titled debut came out in 2002. It's essential listening, showing Tim's increasingly far-reaching ability as a songwriter and arranger, with hip hop, gospel, soul, blues and pop all in the mix. It featured such floor-fillers as 'D.J.' and 'Diamonds And Guns'.

Tim found time to co-write material with Pink for her album *Try This*. The record appeared in November 2003 and featured the smash hit 'Trouble'. It's instantly recognisable as a Tim song, and one could imagine Rancid themselves doing a version. It even won Pink a Grammy. Word at the time was that Pink wanted to rebel against her record company's (Arista) pop roadmap for her. She picked the right ally in Tim then.

The band themselves did manage to record and release new material in 2002, albeit covers of NOFX songs. It was a split release, with NOFX doing versions of Rancid songs, and is covered later in the book.

By the time 2003 arrived, Rancid were a top-level punk band. Their work now had a sophisticated craft that differentiated them from others. Although *Rancid 5* had not sold as well as *Wolves* and *Life*, this was no cause for concern, since it was a hardcore punk release, without the catchy crossover appeal of the previous two albums. It re-established punk rock credibility with the cliquy punk police, though not enough for some. MDC recorded 'Timmy Yo', which was an attack on the success achieved by the likes of Rancid.

Reconvening in 2003, Rancid were free to choose what direction to go in. Punk in 2003 had become very commercial. Pop punk was more pop than punk, with Good Charlotte, Busted, and others riding high. I'm talking melody and catchy hooks with squeaky-clean smiles and bright white teeth. Think 'Rattlesnake'!! Rancid acknowledged this development on *Indestructible*. For the first time, they seemed to respond slightly to the music scene of the day. Smooth pop punk melodies and rap sections were present. *Indestructible* was also easily Rancid's most personal record: not surprising given the events of the preceding three years. It fused the best parts of *Wolves* and *Life*, and to a lesser extent, *Rancid 5*. It mixed sonics nicely – for instance, the twangy 1960s guitar on 'Django' is backed with ferocious punk rock.

Tim took the front cover photo which featured palm trees, telegraph wires and Mohican punk. The red-and-black colour scheme looked edgy. The artwork was by Nick Pritchard from Metro/Sea. The whole thing had a slightly-more-corporate feel about it somehow. Rancid were now definitely – like it or not – big league.

Brett Gurewitz was in the production chair again. Obviously, he knew the band's sound and mentality, and following the hiatus, he was the logical choice. *Indestructible* was recorded in L.A. at the legendary Sound City,

Grandmaster and Sondra Recorders, and was issued on compact disc and double-vinyl album: gorgeous red vinyl, to boot. It came out on Hellcat, but interestingly and contrary to many of their lyrics and apparent philosophy, the band signed a one-off distribution deal with Warner Bros.. This raised a few eyebrows. But the tactic worked. *Indestructible* provided the highest debut chart position of any Rancid album, gate-crashing the *Billboard* chart at number 15. It shifted 51,000 copies in its first week alone.

'Indestructible' (Armstrong, Frederiksen)

This track was inspired by and dedicated to the Ramones: specifically, Joey and Dee Dee. Tim, Matt, Lars, and Brett thought the Ramones album title *Too Tough To Die* was literal: that the Ramones were indeed too tough to die. Music makes you indestructible, and 'Indestructible' pays homage.

Like so many Rancid album-openers, it's to-the-point and fizzing with energy. The rolling chorus – all gritty harmonies – flows over a descending A/F#/D chord sequence. It's reflective, though, as opposed to the usual in-your-face defiance. However, this reflection is put on hold as the track takes a left turn with a sharp halt, a crunching guitar riff, and the arrival of the first verse. This heralds the arrival of Tim's characteristic positivity and defiance. The song *is* called 'Indestructible' after all.

There are several layers here. Obviously, there's material relating to Brody walking out on Tim. Music had already rescued Tim once: as articulated on 'Radio'. Now, in his darkest moments since those early days, it rescued him again. Music gives solace in the grimmest of times. Now, it would save Tim again. The point is, that music can save you, whoever you are. You don't need a mega rock-'n'-roll band behind you.

Play back
Rock and roll come and save me
It's a safe bet
You will never ever betray me

In addition to Joey and Dee Dee Ramone, 'Indestructible' was also dedicated to Joe Strummer. Joe is mentioned in the lyric. His spirit is alive in all of us, and music is salvation. 'And I'll keep listening to the great Joe Strummer/'Cause through music he can live forever'.

However, there is one snarl-up in the words. Rumour had it that Tim and Stza (lead vocalist with New York anarchist ska-punk band Leftover Crack) didn't get on. Tim used to say Stza wasn't even from New York – this is in the second verse: the kid from Avenue A is Stza. Why this was in the lyric, I don't know, but it gives it intrigue and edge. Tim was probably just letting off steam:

See the great Athenians
Man, they're not even from Athens

And the kid from Avenue A
He's not even from Manhattan
And nothing's what it seems

It's quite a lot to pack into one minute and 45 seconds, eh?

'Fall Back Down' (Armstrong, Frederiksen)

Smooth, radio-friendly pop punk tones. Of course, the punk police felt this
was not punk enough for them. Even genuine long-standing Rancid fans are
divided over this number. But they were for much of *Life* too, and that still got
an overall thumbs-up. Not so with 'Fall Back Down'. My theory is it was a little
too close to what several of the lighter-weight pop punk bands were doing,
with its wistful tones floating out of many a radio and being on MTV. The fact
the video featured cameos from Kelly Osbourne and Good Charlotte's Benji
Madden, accentuated these feelings. No one ever had an issue with similar
melodies from bands like Buzzcocks, eh? 'Fall Back Down' was a hit, and is part
of the band's set to this day. It's a song they should be proud of. Just because
you make a record that has obvious commercial appeal, it doesn't mean you're
selling out. Punk is about having the liberty to do exactly what you want,
remember.

It is another defiant lyric, the inspiration being Tim's friendship with the
band members, helping him after splitting from Brody.

I'm very lucky to have my crew
They stood by me when she flew

Rancid's friendship and brotherhood always came first; the band second. This
lyric couldn't say this any clearer. If you fuck with one of us, you fuck with all
of us.

I've always loved the bright, treble-pickup calypso-style guitar sound on Lars'
lead breaks. It's really effective and jumps right out of the mix.

'Red Hot Moon' (Armstrong, Frederiksen, Reed, Aston)

Another highly accessible tune, another huge chorus, and an MTV favourite. It's
a mainstay of the setlist, usually appearing as the closer or during the encore.
This could've easily found a home on *Wolves* or *Life*.

Storytelling makes a welcome return after the personal nature of the opening
two numbers – urban blight, confusion, boredom and a bright young punk
kid (KC) taking a late-night bus ride downtown. KC never felt like she fitted
in, and she trusted no one. She overdosed and was found by the side of a
local baseball pitch and – one assumes – died. The lyric is drenched in druggy
imagery, including flights, haze and the moon – the vision greeting a crystal-
meth addict when the meth is smoked from the inside of an oil-burner pipe. It
leaves a white residue that's moon-like.

But when we found her in the little league park
In the dugout it was cold in the dark
No one knows why she wouldn't wake up
I think she finally made it back home

Rob Aston aka Skinhead Rob gives us a lengthy rap at the end. Aston was a member of Transplants with Tim and Matt, and he co-wrote this number. His contribution to the recording is a lengthy sermon about drugs, temptation, thieving, family and the impact this all has on every aspect of a drug addict's life. Aston's rap adds to the already-strong arrangement, and sets up for the solemn, ghostly, hymn-like final vocal to slowly drift in.

'Red Hot Moon' has a steaming groove, and heat also exists courtesy of the rich organ sound that wraps itself around the track from start to finish: provided once again courtesy of the fabulous Vic Ruggiero. 'Red Hot Moon' works on every level.

'David Courtney' (Armstrong, Frederiksen)

Ladeez and gentlemen, let me pleeze introduce to you the heavyweight champion of California... Mista Lars Frederiksen! On vocals!

The record's fourth cut could've been on *Rancid 5*. It's antagonistic, threatening and dangerous. It also links Lars to the world of London skinhead-gang culture. He's a Millwall F.C. fan whose firm rule is the lion's den of Saturday-afternoon football hooliganism.

David Courtney is a London gangster/author/celebrity. Seriously, don't mess with him. He was mates with the Kray twins and used to proclaim himself to be the most feared man in Britain. He had his nose bitten off and then sewn back on. Vinnie Jones' character in Guy Ritchie's *Lock, Stock and Two Smoking Barrels* was based on Courtney.

Lars' vocal performance is extraordinary. Commanding. Tough. Loud. Intimidating. The track is exactly what's needed to stop the album from sounding too smooth and accessible. It gives *Indestructible,* balance. If you don't agree, I'll send Courtney 'round your place.

'Start Right Now' (Armstrong, Frederiksen)

Glorious pop punk tones return. This is a very-2003 chart punk tune. But it holds up, and shows Tim's vocal versatility. Sure, he could do pop punk. That said, the lyric's plea for unity has Operation Ivy influence. Much of the content here is dreamy, focusing on what Utopia should be like. It analyses what we have and what we should have. Humanity should work together to figure things out, shouldn't it? But this dream-type state is cut in two with a section swiping world leaders for shedding blood across humanity. I love the expletive. It's delivered in such a nonchalant way that keeps the song Rancid-

like, when it could've easily drifted off into Fall Out Boy or Good Charlotte
territory.

> Hostility explodes in the mess, now your arm got blood all over the world
> And clear day turns to dark, blindfolding prisoners of war
> And solidarity, on the razor's edge, what?
> You're a big puncher, right?
> Yeah? Ha! Ha! I don't fuckin' think so

Not that being Good Charlotte is a bad thing, incidentally. Hell, Benji even
appeared in the 'Fall Back Down' video. There is room for everything in a
properly liberal world of punk.

'Out Of Control' (Armstrong, Frederiksen)

The album's balance is restored with another Lars Frederiksen-led assault.
'Out Of Control' sounds, rightly, chaotic. As Tim explored and went down
every musical alley, Lars kept true to his punk rock roots and never particularly
deviated from them. This song underlines this: a song about total attempted
control, despite the title. There are cameras at every ATM, toll booth, traffic
light and roadside across the globe. There is really no escape, or so they think.
It's about resistance and rising up against these controls. The controls are put
there by corruption anyway, so fuck 'em.

  'Out Of Control' is 102 seconds of explosive hardcore – bursting with rage,
alive with pent-up energy and resistance: 'Don't keep questioning IMS/Resist,
resist, resist!'. It says what you need to know.

'Django' (Armstrong)

This merges Ennio Morricone spaghetti-western-style twang guitar with
blistering punk rock, and is one of my favourite sounds on any Rancid record,
anywhere, any time. Matt's bass line is dynamite, and the C#m/G# chord
structure creates a different, edgy feel. The swashbuckling rhythm and sinister
feel, evoke danger, like running from the most dangerous stampede you could
imagine.

  Tim's vocal, slurs over the top, but is completely audible and understandable.
Django was one of the bloodiest spaghetti western films, and we're introduced
to the movie's main character by watching him drag a coffin around the desert.
The film was an influence on the classic Quentin Tarantino-era movies: notably
Reservoir Dogs and *Pulp Fiction*. The band watched many films on the tour
bus: favourites being the horror and spaghetti western genres. The band are
in good company of course: Lee Perry and The Clash were famous spaghetti
western converts.

  Tim's lyric uses the aforementioned *Django* as an analogy for the risks of
taking drugs – you effectively carry your own coffin around with you when you
play the drugs game.

'Arrested In Shanghai' (Armstrong, Frederiksen)

The defiant, rebellious notion behind the lyric is clear: *Stand up when you need to*. From Tiananmen Square, China, to the 14th-century Peasants' Revolt in England, to US Vietnam-war protests, to the UK poll tax demonstrations, populations need to unite and stand up for what they believe in. It's a necessary part of the human psyche, even if you get arrested.

The track is easily the slowest on *Indestructible*. It's even one of the slowest Rancid ever recorded. Vic Rugierro's plinky ghost-like piano, creates an arty noir sonic. This is helped by the A/G#/F#/E chord structure. It's hypnotic minimalism with lots of space and air. However, it's not everyone's favourite Rancid tune, being possibly a little too arty and diverse for some.

'Travis Bickle' (Armstrong, Frederiksen)

Back to the abrasive-sounding Rancid. This is instantly dirty, pummelling and unstoppably high-speed. It's muddy, bloody, lightning punk blues thunder.

Rancid's home from home was New York City. The *Taxi Driver* character Travis Bickle roamed the streets of the Big Apple – the proto-Mohican-punk; the 'quintessential Mohican', to quote the album sleeve notes. Obviously, it's an image punks adopted, including Rancid of course. Lars on the cover of *Wolves*: that could've been Robert De Niro's Bickle, huh? Every Mohican, punk or misfit walking through any red-light district, shopping street or public station in any municipality across the world, could relate to 'Travis Bickle' – the feeling that you don't fit; that everyone's looking at you: especially the cops. Tim's lyric is written from Bickle's frustrated viewpoint; dragged down and kept there by the city's underworld. He roams around it, but is trapped. There's crime, corruption, greed and hatred. It's enough to drive anyone insane.

Game over, it's no fun
Got me on the run
I'm gonna get my gun
Blam blam blam, You're done.

Tim's gnarly, curt vocal, spits the words out with the same contempt Bickle delivers his dialogue in the film – not surprising given the urban blight Tim encountered a decade or so before.

One highlight is the distorted vocal exchange between Tim and Lars. It arrives about 90 seconds in, acting as a bridge to the guitar solo. This is quintessential Rancid.

'Memphis' (Armstrong, Frederiksen)

Joyous stuff. Written in room 122 at a Best Western hotel in Wichita, Kansas, at 3:22 p.m. on 23 June 2003. It was written on tour, and is about being on tour. In the album sleeve notes, Tim stated, 'There's nothing like a highway to make you forget about life's tragedies'. How true this must've been in 2003. One life

Tim knew was that of the touring punk rock musician, and it's possible it was a kind of refuge for him at that point: 'Rolling with the punk rockers/I ain't lying'.

The opening riff is bright and gleaming, like hitting that highway on a sunny day. Optimism, excitement. Synth played by Vic, augments the guitars. This helps with the feeling of freedom. Tim's voice is in fine fettle.

'Spirit Of '87' (Armstrong, Frederiksen, Carlock)

A pounding whirlwind. But the subject matter is dear to every punk fan's heart. It's the unity, warmth and love you get at a gig. You're part of the punk network. Forget your troubles. There are constant references to not ending up at discos on a Saturday night. The track is clearly not anti-disco, it's just that Tim and his kind would rather be at a punk show. It's dedicated to all the venues across the planet who dared put on a punk rock show. So that includes my own place in Leicester, England – The Attik – and its sister joint The Shed. I used to promote shows there under the moniker 101 Productions. Although neither Rancid nor Operation Ivy ever played there, I did put on Vic Ruggiero and The Slackers, US Bombs, The Casualties, Leftover Crack, UK Subs, GDII, Discharge, Cockney Rejects and a multitude of others. So, thank you for this dedication, fellas.

The pace is frenetic, with slashing guitars, raunchy solos, tub-thumping drums and busy bass. The tune spins, slams, and is hedonistic. It also has an anti-violence lyric, singing the praises of the punk rock show, which takes us all away from the shit, violence, corruption and hassles of everyday life. Misfits, homeless folk, the depressed, the disabled; all are welcome.

> Family turns their back on their son
> Now we're all alone
> Now we ain't got a home
> Now we're among our own

Tim and Lars share the vocal, Lars taking the latter half of the second verse, to incredible effect. One final songwriting footnote: 'Spirit Of '87' was co-written by Dave Carlock: an engineer who helped edit the final recording.

'Ghost Band' (Armstrong, Frederiksen)

A breakup song. When you break up with someone, it seems that every band you see, or every song you hear on the radio, has lyrics that relate to you and your ex in every last detail. It's as if it's a ghost. Amazing that, innit? But true. We've all been there. Every word, every metaphor. It relates to her; no escaping it. Thankfully, this song is over in one minute and 37 seconds, otherwise we'd slit our wrists: 'Ghost band, ghost band/There's a ghost band girl playing our songs'.

It's catchy though, with a high-speed tempo and a delicious guitar solo; not to mention the abrupt ending. This all makes this breakup ditty more than bearable, as does the song's humour: a great set of lyrics which are tongue-in-cheek at times.

'Tropical London' (Armstrong, Frederiksen)

This was one of the tracks written and recorded after Brody left Tim, halfway through the making of *Indestructible*. Time was then taken to go away and regroup, and 'Tropical London' – written by Tim and Lars – was one of the seven new songs that resulted.

The track was pushed to radio and MTV. It's obviously commercial, accessible, and to an extent, populist. The ska snap is welcome, and the cut is sequenced in the running order perfectly. It follows a series of predominantly tough and gritty numbers, and alongside 'Memphis', provides balance. It jumps straight in after 'Ghost Band' with hardly a breath taken: I love that kind of thing. The theme of lost love continues, as it's largely about Brody and the emotions Tim was going through: a theme never too far away on this deeply personal record.

> A souvenir reminds me of you
> Every day I catch a glimpse of us too
> I'm the one going through the rescue
> That's why I'm confused you withdrew

Like the reality of hearing certain songs, as articulated in 'Ghost Band', 'Tropical London' reminds Tim of the time he and Brody spent together in cities across the world. Every sign, every souvenir, every sight, can spring up memories after a breakup. Reference is made to Melbourne, Australia: where Brody was born. London was the city where the two spent time. The pain is clear.

> Melbourne is a tropical London
> I met a girl in a tropical London
> Abandoned in tropical London
> Oh no oh no, if you lose me
> You lose a good thing

The backing provides a canvas on which Tim can paint a picture of his heartache. It's subtle, washed with Vic Ruggiero's beautifully sombre keys. The backing vocals – with aahs and woahs aplenty – add texture. The resonant guitar solo continues this. 'Tropical London' is one of Rancid's best-crafted songs.

'Roadblock' (Armstrong, Frederiksen, Reed)

'Roadblock' is the album's second song with a Brett Reed credit. Brett hadn't featured too often as a writer previously but co-wrote this song and 'Red Hot Moon'. It's thumping punk rock lead by Tim and could've easily slotted in on either of Rancid's eponymously titled albums. It again balances the album, after the crafted heartache of 'Tropical London', and gets a few things out of the system in the process. It's one minute and 55 seconds of adrenaline, about the joy of playing live. And how seriously Rancid take it, reflecting the determination and never-say-die mentality of a band getting to a show. In the sleeve notes, the track was dedicated to Motorhead. 'We're not fucking around/ We're not fucking around/We're not fucking around': very Motorhead. These words are the ultimate invitation for a fist-in-the-air sing-along, no? It raises the blood temperature and the hairs on the back of your neck; does you good; gets it out of your system.

'Born Frustrated' (Armstrong, Frederiksen)

High-octane punk rock, this time led by Lars. It's great when a punk band is angry. But if half of them can't write, let alone perform and create a decent song, attitude can only get you so far. Thankfully, Rancid can do all of this. By 2003, they really were expert craftsmen, with the considerable benefit of being able to switch lead vocalists. As the years have moved by, Tim's voice has become more grittily soulful, and Lars' voice has gotten bigger and stronger and more aggressive, shouting out in the name of punk rock. This is all evident on this belter.

This (justifiable) rant is against consumerism, materialism and blind greed. People in so-called developed societies get brainwashed into needing products, so they just go out and buy them. Like sheep being led into a pen, they're drawn onto the shopping-mall escalators and drift aimlessly into the stores. The lyric focuses on both the buyer and the seller. The shops are the dealers, the public the junkies.

> Is it you?
> Is it you that's born frustrated?
> Is this human freedom?
> Hedonistic success?
> Junkie consumerism?
> Mass production, toxic sickness?
> Everyone is wearing now plastic masks that they hide behind
> Marketing massive sales of nothing
> Everything is selling

'Back Up Against the Wall' (Armstrong, Frederiksen)

There are Transplants touches on two of the album's deep cuts, starting here. The chorus is typical Rancid: big, sing-along and easy to grab onto. But the verses allow freestyling, with plenty of air and room to manoeuvre. It's a song for those struggling to make ends meet. Unemployment brings problems: personal, social and obviously financial. Anyone who's been through it, knows this, and the emotions it stirs are deep. The song reflects the sad desperate reality experienced by many.

And she can't be bought, and her nerves are shot
She starts to rot from the inside out
She said I don't need you to save me
But there's people here trying to play me
And there's no jobs that will pay me enough to feed my family

The eagle-eyed among you will have noticed the phrase 'rot from the inside out': like the expression used on the *Rancid* track 'Whirlwind' to describe city life. There's nothing wrong with recycling some of your own lyrics, I'd say. Remember one of 'Midnight Ride's verses was taken into 'Time Bomb'.

Lars takes the bridge later in the track, with Tim's staccato, choppy, hip hop style handling the verse-à la-Transplants.

'Ivory Coast' (Armstrong, Frederiksen)
A punk slammer redresses the equilibrium. Its blistering speed, flies round the Eb/Bb/F/Gm structure: not a sequence used too many times in the band's career thus far. Tim's gravel voice is clear as a bell and high in the mix.

'Ivory Coast' is the album's one direct reference to world politics. The first civil war in the West African nation of Cote d'Ivoire (Ivory Coast) ran from 2002 to 2004. On New Year's Eve 2002, a brief ceasefire was permitted, both sides being allowed to *celebrate* the turning of the year. French soldiers on the side of Laurent Gbagbo's government, were drinking champagne, and fired rifles into the air. The next day, they were told that anyone found outside after dark would be shot: the ludicrous contradictory nature of the war.

These lyrics show Tim carrying the Strummer torch forward. Following Joe's passing, someone needed to continue to bring global issues to the attention of the punk masses. There's no better way than writing songs about them, especially well-crafted, catchy ones.

They'll shoot ya down, right on sight
If you're out at the wrong time of night
And in a civil war, there's no civil rights

The track is a Rancid bullet, with no fat, and is very succinct.

'Stand Your Ground' (Armstrong, Frederiksen)
One of the band's best deep cuts, and there are quite a few of these, as you may be realising. The song is dedicated to those without a home and forced to live on the streets.

So, when you've got no place to sleep at night
And you're all huddled up and you're cold
Well, this song goes out to city's forgotten

The lyric focuses on homelessness in Los Angeles. Tim put it succinctly in the sleeve notes: 'We focused on L.A. in this song, and even though the sun shines most of the time, Los Angeles can be so fucking cold'.

This is the second of the tracks showing the Transplants touch – in the verse vocal, where Tim delivers in a staccato, part-spoken, part-sung way. The roomy, cool backing allows this. The track's whole sonic has a gritty slickness, incorporating delicious twangy rock-'n'-roll guitar parts which cut through the well-oiled sound. This gives the track an edge it might otherwise lack, and prevents it from being too sanitised, thankfully. The chorus swoops majestically, with Tim's solo tones simply wonderful. *Live life to the fullest* is the message, despite any tough circumstances. You never know what might happen to you next.

'Otherside' (Armstrong, Frederiksen)

Speaking of which, *Indestructible* ends with another intensely personal song. This time it's Lars' turn to articulate his emotions, in a brilliant song co-written with his brother from another mother: Tim Armstrong. Lars tragically lost his blood-brother Rob in 2001.

Ask Rancid fans for their favourite track on the album, and many will plump for this one. It's a high-energy, in-your-face delivery, and a classic Lars vocal. Despite the tragic theme, the whole thing leaves the listener in a positive frame. Punk rock is all about positivity. We all should be grateful Lars' big brother introduced him to punk rock music and culture. As a result of this, we've been able to revel in the presence of the movement's most charismatic, approachable and talented stars. We should thank Rob for this and celebrate his life with 'Otherside'. That is positivity, I'd say. The affection for Robert is obvious in the verse lyric:

I miss the days that you walked with me
Loyal brother, loyal friend
Showed me how to be a man
I love Robert and I always will

The first time Rancid played the song live – at Sonara – there wasn't a dry eye in the house. To have such a lyric written in tribute to a departed loved one, and to then put the words to such a pulsating punk soundtrack, is quite something. It's an obituary and love song played exactly as – one senses – Rob would've wanted it. The fact both Lars and Tim sing the lines solo, adds to the depth of feeling: depth that can only be found with real, true brotherhood and friendship. And that, of course, is at the heart of Rancid.

Contemporary Releases
'Fall Back Down'/'Killing Zone' (7" single)
Release date: 2003, Chart positions: UK: 42, US: 13
This single stayed on the *Billboard* chart for 11 weeks.

A-side
'Fall Back Down' (Armstrong, Frederiksen)
This is the album version.

B-side
'Killing Zone' (Armstrong, Frederiksen)
This appeared on the *B-Sides And C-Sides* and *Essentials* compilations. It was also the lead track on the fourth *Give 'Em The Boot* compilation. It is quite *metal* in its sound, especially the chorus – an example of the band reacting to the world around them, as metal and punk moved closer together after the turn of the century.

The song is more about the war being fought on the streets, I'd say, not an actual war. However, street war can lead to civil and even regional war. There isn't that much difference – killing is killing, whatever the scale. The message is, *Care for those close to you.*

> Head straight to the killing zone, now the war is on
> Hold on to yours or we're all gone

'Fall Back Down'/'Killing Zone'/'Stranded' (CD single)
This has the same detail as the 7", but with an additional track.

'Stranded' (Armstrong, Frederiksen)
'Stranded' has a wonderfully crisp Tim vocal. The backing is pummelling, but with a softer production compared to both *Rancid* albums: something indicative of the *Indestructible* era. It's a sentimental song about Tim's old 1962 Fender acoustic guitar. This went with him everywhere, and this is the tale 'Stranded' tells.

> Where do I begin?
> To tell you what we've seen
> Together all over the world
> Could not make it without you

'Tropical London' (Armstrong, Frederiksen)
Release Date: 2003, Chart position: Did not chart
A CD promo to US radio. The album version.

'Red Hot Moon' (Armstrong, Frederiksen, Reed, Aston)
Release Date: 2003, Chart position: Did not chart
CD promo edited for radio purposes. In other words, censored by expletives being removed.

Indestructible (Expanded edition) (2015)
This expanded edition added 'Killing Zone' and 'Stranded' to the track listing.

Let The Dominoes Fall (LP) (2009)

Personnel:
Tim Armstrong, Lars Frederiksen: guitar, vocal
Matt Freeman: bass, vocals
Branden Steineckert: drums
Label: Hellcat
Producer: Brett Gurewitz
Release dates: UK: 1 June 2009, US: 2 June 2009
Chart positions: US: 11, UK: 41
Running time: 45:39

Punk rock at the onset of the digital and social-media age, mirrored society. There was lots on offer, and you had to dig through it to get to the good stuff. New acts were plentiful, and with the online platforms, a new band could get a following in a fraction of the time spent putting on and promoting shows. Downloading music became the new norm. It was cheaper and took up less physical storage space. And this new medium allowed an act to include a whole host of bonus tracks.

Across the punk rock network, however, many old-school methods still worked – tours, and especially festivals. More Punk Rock Bowling and Lollapalooza-style fests seemed to appear every summer. Musically, many new punk acts had a metallic element to their work. In the UK, a hot new band like Enter Shikari found themselves headlining tours and rising higher up the bill at Download and Reading festivals. In the States, Rise Against had moved on from Fat Wreck Chords, signed to a major and subsequently sold more units. The nostalgia circuit was going from strength to strength. The reformed Sex Pistols played some of their best live shows ever, at London's Brixton Academy in 2008. Countless other legends were now reunited, cramming venues and filling outdoor bills the world over.

Overall, there seemed room for everybody and everything as the 2000s progressed. Thankfully, established punk rock giants – which now certainly included Rancid and associated side projects – profited. *Indestructible* had given Rancid their highest *Billboard* chart position. Both Transplants LPs also got into the *Billboard* top 100. Meanwhile, Green Day enjoyed massive global success with *American Idiot* in 2004, and were now up there with the likes of U2, vying for world domination.

Rancid's touring schedule on the back of *Indestructible* was extensive, with them often inviting a legendary act to share the stage: like Birmingham legends GBH. Tim knew his band's status and used this to ensure that his fans were fully aware of punk's heritage.

There was a six-year gap between *Indestructible* and its follow-up. In 2005, Transplants issued *Haunted Cities*, with distribution through Atlantic. It was a success, and the band toured, featuring on several of the Warped travelling rock tours. The DJ, gospel, rock and hip hop crossover was cutting edge, with one foot paying homage, the other forging new ground.

Lars Frederiksen and the Bastards issued their second album *Viking* on Hellcat in 2004. It was a punk rock record through and through. Lars would do nothing different: he lived and breathed punk. Most of the album was co-written with Tim, including the cathartic 'The Viking': about Lars' brother Rob.

In 2007, Tim dropped the solo album *A Poet's Life*: a collection of reggae tracks. Lively dancehall ('Into Action') sat next to roots tunes ('Inner City Violence'), and if it weren't for Tim's gritty vocal, one could've been forgiven for not realising it was by him at all. Matt's psychobilly project Devils Brigade issued the debut single 'Stalingrad' b/w 'Psychos All Around Me' in 2003. The follow-up 'Vampire Girl' appeared in 2005. Featuring Matt on double bass and vocals, plus Tim and Lars, it was very much a Rancid-family project.

But there were other reasons for the long gap. In May 2005, Matt Freeman was diagnosed with lung cancer. Fortunately, after surgery in June, it was concluded that his condition was not terminal, and – judging by his titanic live performances – Matt appears to have made a complete recovery since. However, back in 2005, Transplants obviously had to cancel plenty of dates, including a Warped Tour.

There was yet another significant factor in the delay. After 15 years behind the drum kit, Brett Reed quit. He'd joined Rancid as a novice, and Tim and Matt were patient with him as he got up to speed. Rancid developed a unique rhythmic style. Brett's playing had swing to it. In 1998 he told the webzine *In Music We Trust*: 'This was like, my first band. I hadn't even played drums for five months when I ran into Tim'. Brett always seemed to go with the flow, enjoying the benefits of the band's success and becoming able to help out his family, which meant a lot to him. But he was not enamoured with the show business side of being in a band: 'Show business is fucked. The media warps everything ... After six years in a band, I've experienced a lot of that ... My advice for any band is to choose close friends, and make decisions that are best for yourself'.

Brett co-wrote two songs on *Indestructible;* his songwriting credits had been rare beforehand. It was rumoured he wasn't happy about the band signing a distribution deal with Warner for the album. The band had a nice long holiday after touring *Indestructible*, and it's quite conceivable that Brett didn't want to commit to another long round of recording and touring which would've meant more time away from home and family.

Brett's contribution to Rancid was huge, and it's difficult to see how the brotherhood could've evolved without him. The Gilman skater-punk kid had gone a long way with his buddies. He did well for them, and by them. And then he was gone. All his social media accounts are private, and he's given no interviews since his departure. As far as anyone can tell, Rancid remains his one-and-only band.

Let The Dominoes Fall arrived in 2009 and will be referred to as *Dominoes* from hereon. The gap was partially plugged with the superb 2007 *B-Sides And C-Sides* compilation in 2007. More on this later.

Brett's replacement was in place quickly. Branden Steineckert was a founder member of The Used, and in fact left that band three months prior to Tim tracking him down. Branden posted on his *Twitter* in 2015: 'I was kicked out of my band The Used for my sober/drug-free lifestyle. These guys (Rancid) were there for me when I got knocked down. I was happy that I could be there for them'. Instantly there appeared kinship and camaraderie. The first Rancid album Branden played on was *Dominoes*. Rancid's highest-charting LP, it reached 11 on the *Billboard* chart. So, the break seemed to do Rancid no harm in the popularity stakes.

The album is quite different from those that went before. It starts slowly compared to the exploding opening cuts on the previous half dozen albums. Tim's continued musical evolution – notably with Transplants – was obvious on many tracks. Furthermore, *Dominoes* is the only Rancid album with a group photograph on the cover – albeit in a punk Xerox style, but still a photograph, taken by Mitch Ikeda. There was even a poster shoved inside the packaging. Design and artwork was again by Nick Pritchard at Metro/Sea. Like all their previous LPs, it was released in a double-vinyl format in a gatefold sleeve. Another first (with one exception) was all songwriting being credited to Rancid, rather than to the individual songwriters.

Production was again by Gurewitz, and the recording was spread between L.A.'s Bloodclot, Sound City and Jhoc studios, and George Lucas' Skywalker Sound in San Francisco. Plenty of guest musicians appeared on the album, and though there were not as many as on *Life*, these will be listed under individual tracks. Mainstay Slacker Vic Ruggiero was again present, amidst the mandolin, violin and cello: instruments hinting that this album was going to sound different to previous Rancid records.

Dominoes got mixed reviews. When the band's albums are ranked by various fanzines, websites and in magazine articles, *Dominoes* is often in ninth position (last). In my view, this reflects the quality of all Rancid's LPs rather than any shortcomings on the part of *Dominoes*. As the excellent music blogger *Brooklyn Vegan* put it in 2019: 'Rancid don't have any bad albums, and even their worst is pretty good, and *Let The Dominoes Fall* is pretty good'.

'East Bay Night' (Rancid)

Unusually for Rancid, the opener has a steady tempo rather than the stereotypical blistering assault. This song is easy to fall in love with. The evocative lyric recalls growing up in the East Bay. It's about playing Gilman Street, hanging out, friends and family. Roots. Matt told the band's Myspace page in 2009: 'Writing about the Bay Area, always came easy to us. In so many ways you are where you came from: it's ingrained in you. It can shape you and define you'.

When the band were completing *Dominoes*, they realised more songs were needed, and quickly wrote 'East Bay Night'. It's part-shanty, most definitely punk, and with a hint of folk in its story. There's a bass solo too. Matt played a 1977

Fender Precision he'd had for over 20 years. In the high register, it struggled to stay in tune. This came through on playback, and Brett Gurewitz insisted that the solo be redone. Tim refused. Punk rock: the freedom to do what you want.

The duelling middle section has a real punk rock feel. Matt plays the scales, and Tim does the same on the octaves. It's frenetic stuff; mad but never out of control. East Bay chemistry, you see. Tim explained, again on the band's Myspace: 'I've been playing music with Matt for 25 years and have known him since first grade. There's a deep connection between us. So when we play music together, that deep connection comes across'. It's easy to overlook this. 'East Bay Night' seems an appropriate moment to remind ourselves.

Branden slotted right into this already well-oiled machine. Immediately it's clear he's a seasoned drummer, his deep tom-tom rolls powering the chorus.

The track was included as the opener on Hellcat's *Give 'Em The Boot Volume 7*, released in 2009.

'This Place' (Rancid)

This track could've been on *Let's Go* and could've even been the traditional blistering opening cut on *Dominoes*. It's high-octane stuff, ripping out of the blocks and staying out in front. But it's anthemic, rather than raw punk: a decent analysis of the majority of *Dominoes*.

The lyric is inspired by America's rust belt – part of the North-Eastern and Mid-Western states that have been in industrial decline since the 1980s. It describes the towns and cities that make up the region, and how their heart and soul were ripped out, leaving only a carcass behind.

> The coal's on the fire
> Ain't burning no more
> In the lake shore foundries
> The workers misled by corporations
> That knows no boundaries
> This place is a tale of horror
> This place is a ghost town now

'Up To No Good' (Rancid, Gurewitz)

Naughty, toe-tapping ska. 'Up To No Good' has a 2 Tone English feel – especially the Hammond organ solo played by Stax keyboard legend Booker T. Jones. Jones was in town working on an album for Hellcat's sister label Anti. His presence on *Dominoes* was quite a coup for Rancid. In 2009, Matt Freeman described the scene in the studio:

> One of the best parts besides watching Booker play, was watching all the starstruck studio engineers. These guys are all old hands who've seen everything, but Booker's playing was that impressive. We are very lucky to have him on our record.

The lyric provides a candle for those who have nothing and describes what they have to do to survive. Robbin' and ransackin'. Bobbin' and weavin'. Lars Frederiksen elaborated on Myspace in 2009: 'The natures of those who play the game of survival, are not for us to judge, but only to observe'.

The warm brass gives the cut further texture. A popular hit in punk clubs across the world, its 2-Tone snap and groove of course resonates to this day.

'Last One To Die' (Rancid)

A proper anthem, and one of Rancid's last *Billboard* chart singles at the time of writing. However, the critical response was mixed. No one had any qualms with the anthemic characteristics with a big chorus and its passionate delivery. But a few seemed to take issue with the lyric's self-congratulatory nature. In 2009, *Punk News* referred to its 'rather narcissistic appraisal of the band's longevity'. Certainly, the lyric does seem to point the finger at those who sneered at Rancid at times. Remember, as the punk movement splintered into more subgenres, Rancid were the last true punk band standing. They had the image, the gritty sound and the defiant provocative stance. The song's chorus seemed to wind people up: 'We only listen to the words that we sing/Now a million are singing along'. It's a song about survival. Tim said in 2009: ''The Last One To Die' is about the survival of our band. Over the last 18 years, we've seen a lot of bands and friends pass on, quit, or move on for various reasons, yet we keep moving forward'.

Apparently, the song came together in a jam at the end of a day's recording. It's immediate, in the key of G major, steady-paced with brightly distorted guitars and a solid-as-a-rock rhythm track. Celebratory, for sure. Maybe that's why it sounds so anthemic. Branden, who helped with backing vocals, described the track in 2009 as 'Oi! music meets Bruce Springsteen'. Somewhere between Cockney Rejects and The Boss, then. Cool.

'Disconnected' (Rancid)

Dominoes is an album of firsts for Rancid. Another one is all three lead vocalists singing lead on the same track. 'Disconnected' is one such track. Lars takes the first verse, Tim the second and Matt the third. It's another big tune that originated in acoustic form in another jam session. The theme is self-explanatory. Disconnection happens on a personal level from time to time. You move away from your hometown, and feel the link between you and your friends, family and past life has been broken. Furthermore, you can become disconnected from your country. In America, public schooling teaches the pledge of allegiance and what it means to be a patriot. However, as time moves on, some covet this, and others rebel against it: disconnection from the country you love.

Branden thumps out a raw Sham 69-style rhythm in the final chorus. I love such homages to the late-1970s punk bands I grew up with in England. Sham 69 are a band who have influenced so many, and their working-class honesty obviously appeals to Rancid. Of course, Rancid covered 'If The Kids Are United', and Branden's later-chorus drum pattern borrows from this Sham classic.

'I Ain't Worried' (Rancid)
And the English influence doesn't stop with Sham 69. Again, there is an early-2 Tone sound lurking in the backing: reminiscent of The Beat's 'Mirror In The Bathroom'. There's also a Dee Dee Ramone touch to Matt's bass-playing. Dee Dee's fast root-note up-down right-hand picking is harder to do than it looks, and is used cleverly behind the busy 'Mirror In The Bathroom' rhythm. Thus, Rancid doff their cap to two underground music legends.

The chorus vocal delivery is tonally deep; Tim bringing a contemporary slant as he sings: 'I ain't worried about a goddamn thing/I hear them talking, I ain't listening'.

In a 2009 interview, Lars referred to the influence of another Englishman: the poet Linton Kwesi Johnson: 'I think the chorus says it all. In the vein of Linton Kwesi Johnson, just sped up some'. Johnson's rhythmic poetry carried the fight in 1970s/1980s England, when racism was rife. His contribution to the social and musical landscape is colossal and should be investigated by all. I reckon Lars was referring to Johnson's vocal delivery. Obviously, unity and equality are what Rancid have always been about.

I don't give a fuck is clearly the sentiment behind the lyrics elsewhere. Each lead singer gets the chance to put in a vocal rap: quite something in Matt Freeman's case:

I'm Matt Freeman, I'm coming in quick
I got a 6-4 Merc and a clutch that won't slip
I don't give a goddamn what they say
I'm born and raised in the East Bay

Can't argue with any of that, eh? However, the last verse – delivered by Lars – is the most pertinent:

Black, brown, white, we're all punk rock
We're the kings of the low-income block
Worn-out sneakers, skinheads, mohawks
When we all get together, yeah the music won't stop

It reminds me of 'Unity' by Operation Ivy. Linton Kwesi Johnson would surely approve.

'Damnation' (Rancid)
Fast, pumping punk rock, in G major. It's not as raw and hardcore as on either self-titled *Rancid* album but is certainly punk enough for *Let's Go*. Big sound, big energy, big passion.

The Chuck Berry-style guitar in the chorus is always welcome, working alongside the chant of 'Damnation' against a backdrop of D/G chords. The deep gang-style background vocals are effective and involve Pat Wilson from Weezer and Bad Religion's Greg Graffin.

The lyric focuses on society's slump after times of prosperity. Hotels and motels that once were so appealing and open for business, are now run down and often boarded up.

Hotel building, all the machines are broken down
It's a narrow path between evil and good
Watch the strong man in his decline
Another man dying is misunderstood

'New Orleans' (Rancid)

This is possibly the album's best track. Lars Frederiksen makes a welcome return as lead vocalist. His huge voice just sounds so right on big full-on numbers, and his gusto dominates this track. The melody is strong, and you'll be singing it in your head all day. Lars' singing is supported by fantastic backing vocals: the crafted 'woah''s sounding almost Beach Boys-like.

The stripped-down final verse underlines the poignant theme, and it's a serious one. The band – like all people with heart and a sense of culture and fun – love New Orleans. Its energy and people are unlike anywhere else on Earth. So when Hurricane Katrina hit the city in 2005 – leaving over 1800 fatalities and untold damage to lives and properties – everyone who ever visited or loved the place, recoiled in horror and said a prayer. This song is about the protagonist's relationship with New Orleans, his love and feelings for the city, and his reaction when the hurricane hit. To articulate this, Rancid provide a sentimental tearjerking lyric, presented in a vibrant high-velocity punk rock number. It's something they do regularly: remember 'Otherside' from the last record?

'Civilian Ways' (Rancid)

This one is a real departure, and easily the most experimental thing on the album. It has a folky Americana feel with its acoustic backing, slow easy tempo, mandolin, brushed snare and hushed low-fi vocals. The mandolin was played by Ryan Foltz from Dropkick Murphys, incidentally. The rootsy, bluesy slide guitar work is wonderful, as is Vic Ruggiero's subtle keys work. The instrumental break consisting of a mandolin solo superseded by a sparse guitar fits the mood, and is dreamlike. Matt Freeman plays upright bass.

Tim's vocal is particularly heartfelt, the subject matter being his brother Greg, his family and thousands like them. Greg got Tim into punk rock, but it's Greg's time in the military that's behind 'Civilian Ways'. Greg spent a year in Iraq, where he needed eyes in the back of his head just to stay alive. The lyric was inspired by this hyper-alert state, coupled with Tim and the family's worries about Greg being out there, and finally Greg's return home and subsequent struggle to adapt to civilian life: 'May we never forget the sacrifices my friends made for me'. Heartfelt stuff, and a new avenue in Tim's songwriting. He told the *L.A. Times* in 2009: 'When we went into Iraq, our country wasn't at war, 150,000 families were. It's hard to talk about, so this is my way of telling my family that I love them'.

'The Bravest Kids' (Rancid)

The military theme continues – people who go overseas and fight, doing their duty, trying to improve situations; being part of something they believe in. All of this when so much in life is wasted on so little. 'The bravest kids I know, are the ones that got to go fighting over there'.

The fast tempo wasn't the original plan. It took a couple of different forms before a traditional Rancid approach was taken. Maybe due to the lyric's deep nature, alternative formats were attempted. However, to have another rootsy slice of Americana so soon, would've left the album a little unbalanced. Alternate and experimental sequencing had by and large served Rancid so well on their previous albums, so why change it?

It's anthemic rather than gritty: an overall feature of *Dominoes*. It has a huge chorus, with well-crafted backing vocals. Branden's drum fills are fantastic, particularly prior to the second chorus. Already, his powerful playing was taking the band to a different level, and certainly gave Matt a new sparring partner.

'Skull City' (Rancid)

On this sleazy rocker, Tim's voice sounds like it's coming from deep down in the gravel pit. This has a proper barroom feel – pool tables, table dancers and bottles of beer spilling all over the soundscape.

Evidently, it was inspired by the England Northern Soul movement and the working-class demographic it attracted. Wooden floors sprinkled with talcum powder to facilitate elaborate, energetic dancing and partying; keep the faith and live for the weekend: all that kind of stuff. The sound of the working poor in the bars, clubs and venues, all dripping with sweat, reeking of smoke. Some cities live and others die, but people keep them alive at the weekend. I take the dancing girl as a metaphor for those hardworking folk who keep those weekends alive for the rest of us.

> She's my go-go baby
> She's my honky-tonk girl
> She dances on my table
> She dances on a pole

'L.A. River' (Rancid)

Hooray for a Matt Freeman lead vocal. It's very punk rock, as in doing exactly what you want to do and fuck whatever anyone else thinks about it. A belter.

Matt's vocal is typically uncompromising. His growl and commitment are without equal, and in punk music, this counts more than anything else. The 'boomshakalalalaboom shimmy-shimmy-shimmy' in the chorus, is something to comprehend. The remaining chorus vocal is almost crooned in unison by the backing singing, which gives the track a nice vocal juxtaposition.

There is great rockabilly guitar too, especially the descending riff over the G chord: think 'Runaway Boys' by Stray Cats.

The theme is Los Angeles. So many people arrive in the City of Angels, trying to make a life, but it doesn't work out. So they end up being dragged down into street life, drugs and crime, and eventually move away, or worse: pass away. The L.A. river – not the world's most spectacular waterway – is a metaphor. It carries the dreams of these people away, and they are now left with a disappointed reality.

'Lulu' (Rancid)

Serious social comment, reflecting the plight of single-parent families: particularly mothers. Their financial hardships and struggles trying to make ends meet, are reflected all over the world. Lulu is a single parent. Her partner, we discover, is in the armed forces, stationed in Iraq and then Afghanistan. He ain't coming back. Therefore, Lulu is on her own, having to raise her family and pay the bills, doing whatever she has to do.

> Lulu works all day long
> She goes nine-to-five just to stay alive
> She'll do anything just to walk the line
> There ain't no time to wine and dine
> Wartime now in the USA
> And her husband goes far away
> Afghanistan and Iraq
> Her husband now ain't coming back

The arrangement is well put together – a funky spacey chorus interspersed with a massively-overdriven and powerful guitar-based verse. The key is Ab, unusually. Thus, there's lots of light and shade. The chorus instrumentation is a rimshot rhythm, clean, close-up guitar, a melodic bass pattern, and not much else except for the title being softly sung.

'Dominoes Fall' (Rancid)

Effectively the album's title track, this is quite modish, with Vic Ruggiero's keyboards giving a full Secret Affair or *Sound Effects*-era Jam sound, with a touch of The Lurkers to keep things punk. Again, a UK influence.

The lively major-chord riff with twangy second-guitar licks and chanted 'na-na-na''s, add to the bright feel. The riff is actually very similar to the chorus riff on 'Lulu', only fuller, with light and warm distortion and a Pete Townsend guitar approach. It works well sequenced after 'Lulu', with both tracks being similar tempo-wise, and sharing danceable mod rhythms.

The theme, is *Don't force things*. What will be, will be. Let the dominoes fall the way they will. 'Dominoes Fall' was written after dinner, shortly after the band decamped to Skywalker Sound in San Francisco.

'Liberty And Freedom' (Rancid)

This is a strutting, boss reggae cut in the spirit of 1969. Reggae is of course rebel music, and was adopted by punks when the likes of Don Letts started spinning Jamaican sounds at The Roxy in London in 1976. Punk A-listers such as John Lydon and Paul Simonon were already reggae fans, growing up in London with the offspring of the Windrush generation. Soon, every punk was also a reggae fan. And so of course, was Tim. And with *A Poet's Life*, he was now a reggae musician. 'Liberty and Freedom' carries a protest lyric, rather like a folk song. The words make direct attacks, and are easy to fathom and understand. Tim made the lyric's theme clear in 2009 on the band's Myspace. 'Plain and simple, it's about the systematic suppression of ideas, and censorship. It's also a protest song in the folk tradition of Woody Guthrie'.

I like the message behind this song. It isn't just a rant about how unfair things are. There are those of us who take our liberty and freedom seriously and do stuff to ensure it remains. The threat is not just an *enemy*, it's the authorities who we supposedly trust. So if someone apparently harmlessly sprays graffiti with a message threatening action, maybe we should heed what that person has said, rather than listen to the authorities who condemn the act? Because one day that splash of graffiti may become action, and not just a slogan.

Liberty and freedom
In quotations spraypainted on the wall
Verbalised explosions
We will come back some day

'If You Want It, You Got It' (Rancid)

Another three-vocalist song. It's a wonder Rancid took until their seventh album to get around to doing it. This is a song very much about the unifying nature of punk rock – particularly at a show, like on 'Spirit of '87'. Right from the Op Ivy days, Matt and Tim have written tunes about unity in all aspects of life.

Spiky UK hardcore heroes GBH are immortalised further in the lyric. Being name-checked by the biggest-selling street-punk band of all time, is an accolade.

Some live a life of indecision
Strung out in the petty schism

I heard GBH, I made a decision
Punk rock is my religion

The track rushes on through to a brief pause, courtesy of a sole guitar and
vocal, then back to a final thrust. It's over in just under 100 seconds.

'Locomotive' (Rancid)
Continuing the previous track's tempo, 'Locomotive' is fast – an express train
of a track if you'll pardon the pun. This crashing cut has panache, and is the
closest *Dominoes* gets to the high-octane sound of the *Rancid* albums. But it
would be more at home on *Let's Go*. A feature of this track is Lars' lead guitar
work. It jumps out, all bridge-pickup and piercing-through amidst a barrage of
rock-'n'-roll licks over a D/A/C/G chord structure. Tasty.

'Just The Way It Is Now' (Rancid)
A thrusting, thumping reggae stomper: the second of two amidst the *Dominoes*
deep cuts. The track also contains Dynamites-style brass lines, and dub
sound-effects. It's a veritable mix of Jamaican recording techniques mashed
together by Tim, whose slurred part-sung, part-toasted verse, sits on top. Vic
Ruggiero's keys provide wash, but the wah-wah guitar solo stops the track from
disappearing too much into the dancehall. It reminds us that it's indeed Rancid
we're listening to, and not something from Orange Street, Kingston. But, like
'Liberty and Freedom', it does lack the band's usual abrasive touch present on
their other reggae tracks.

The lyric is about going along with society's rules: written and unwritten. It's
about being unprepared to take a risk and walk the path you want or dream of,
and therefore denying yourself freedom. It paraphrases Joe Strummer in the
process: 'First rule, they always sell/Second rule, never tell/Third rule, straight
to hell'. The message encourages us to be punk and take that risk.

'The Highway' (Rancid)
Dominoes closes with a second slice of Americana. 'The Highway' features
acoustic instrumentation and a drooling, endearing vibe of friendship, hope
and travel. The song is a sequel to the *Indestructible* tracks 'Spirit of '87',
'Memphis' and 'Roadblock'. It's about the nomadic life of a band – the life Tim,
Lars, Matt, and now Branden, have chosen. However, rather than show this in
a punk rock number, Rancid take an intimate, campfire approach, and in doing
so, had to put 'The Highway' as the album's last song.

The band's friendship has of course always been the single-most-important
thing. Branden wouldn't have been chosen if Tim, Lars and Matt didn't think
he had the potential to recognise this and become part of the brotherhood.
The track reflects this warmth.

The friendship theme has a second part – the band playing music to their
friends in the audience. Friendship is all-important in punk. Camaraderie.

It's also a song of hope – the hope that Rancid and others like them can keep doing what they love: keep playing music to their friends. The working classes have so much struggle, so much strife – so it's a remedy for all of us.

> I am working-class culture
> Seen on the bleak side of the American experience
> Scatter in the streets and show me what you got
> This is no set of ideas, this is flesh and blood

Tim – always a humble guy – is grateful for his lot. This is all he's done and all he wants to keep doing. He could've ended up in so many other places, including dark ones. The words make so much sense, and the chorus is self-explanatory.

> Nightclubs and one-night stands
> Play a show then I'm off again
> This is my life on the highway
> It's all I've ever done, all I've ever known
> Just wanna play one more show
> Play some music with my friends

The harmonica, acoustic guitars and bass, wrap themselves around the words, which Tim delivers in rugged country-punk fashion. The lyric's touch of sadness, the uncertainty of the working classes and the loneliness of one-night stands, give the song a bleak edge. Otherwise, it would be a little too cringy, maybe? It is Rancid we're talking about, not Bon Jovi. Either way, brotherhood runs true, and working-class culture, rules, right?

Contemporary Releases
'Last One To Die' (CD single, Promo)
Release date: 2009, Chart positions: US: 22, UK: Did not chart
Same as the album version. Issued in the US, Japan and Europe. It spent 12 weeks on the *Billboard* chart.

'Up To No Good' (CD single, Promo)
US Release Date: 2009, Chart position: Did not chart
A US release only, censored for radio purposes.

Let The Dominoes Fall (Expanded edition) (2009)
The is the most interesting of all the expanded album editions. It includes a disc of acoustic recordings, plus a DVD on the making of the album. As this book focuses on Rancid's music, I will deal with the acoustic disc, again produced by Brett Gurewitz.

'East Bay Night' (Rancid)

A simple guitar and vocal demo. The song's natural strum-and-sing-along campfire feel is obvious, and thus there's no need to change the vocal approach.

'L.A. River' (Rancid)

A great version, with acoustic backing including a full acoustic drum kit. A large cast of unplugged instruments add considerably to the arrangement, which includes banjos (Mark Switzer, Matt Hensley), accordion (Robert Hoehn, Justin Gorski), piano (Gorski) and harmonica (Patrick French). Matt's voice sounds fantastic and is well-suited to the rustic-folk drive. It sounds like a gang of cowboys making a getaway: a good thing.

'I Ain't Worried' (Rancid)

Another large line-up of instruments. Thumping bass drum drives things on. It retains the dark defiant threat of the album recording, and all three vocalists get their moment again. The mandolin, piano and banjo contribute superbly, adding melodic flurries, especially later on after Lars' final vocal.

'This Place' (Rancid)

Stripped back; just one guitar and vocal. Close-up, demo-style.

'Disconnected' (Rancid)

There's a bright country sound to the arrangement. The three distinct vocalists come through with even more clarity. It's subtle, with limited percussion and an accordion accompanying guitar and bass.

'Liberty And Freedom' (Rancid)

Beautiful, wistful mandolin played by Ryan Foltz gives a dreamy quality matching the lyric's prophetic nature. Lars' electric guitar provides a cutting edge. It's not acoustic reggae, incidentally, but more dark-and-rugged country.

'Dominoes Fall' (Rancid)

This is quite contemporary and poppy. Loud, smacking percussion provides the backbeat, with an amazing slide guitar solo at the end.

'New Orleans' (Rancid)

An exhilarating opening to one of the best *Dominoes* songs is stripped back, with limited backing, but still sounds fantastic. Lars' voice is restrained, fitting in with the airy feel.

There's light and shade in line with the original arrangement, busy bass at times, and up-tempo clapping setting the rhythm.

'You Want It, You Got It' (Rancid)
This features an accordion high in the mix, and a delicious rolling bass line. The three vocalists are to the fore again, which are even more evident when the arrangement is so bare.

'Outgunned' (Rancid)
Previously unreleased and a new song to most fans. The lyric is about the punk network. Survival and unity matter more than numbers, as the chorus states: 'Always outnumbered, never outgunned'. The song has a swooping, majestic quality with Tim and Lars' interchanging vocals. Obviously, it would be interesting to hear an electric version: something that – to my knowledge – has never been released, even on a live bootleg.

'The Bravest Kids' (Rancid)
This sounds cool. It's simple, with a sharp harmonica break and plenty of room in the mix. Tim's gravelly voice, suits, and the subtle skilful vocal harmonies float around beautifully. A highlight.

'Last One to Die' (Rancid)
This is tambourine and bass-drum driven, with terrific banjo work from Switzer and Hensley. Matt Hensley is a member of Celtic punk band Flogging Molly, incidentally. Again, the vocal harmonies are terrific, adding to the song's triumphant, defiant nature. Magic.

...Honor Is All We Know (LP) (2014)

Personnel:
Tim Timebomb (Armstrong), Lars Frederiksen: guitar, vocals
Matt Freeman: bass, vocals
Branden Steineckert: drums
Label: Hellcat
Producer: Brett Gurewitz
Release date: 27 October 2014
Chart positions: US: 20, UK: 45
Running time: 32:53

By 2014, Rancid had been together for 23 years (over three times longer than The Clash), and were considered as veterans of the punk rock world. New scenesters incorporated metal, electronica and other elements, and reached millions of followers with a click. To think I used to look forward all week to going to a record shop on a Saturday morning to spend my hard-earned pocket money on one 7" record.

Speaking of singles, these veterans released 46 of them in 2012, making up the *Essentials* compilation. Yes, 46 of them. A cracking item, but god it was expensive to buy. It will be covered later.

Back to the punk scene in 2014. How did Rancid fit in? Some young hipsters sneered at Rancid's hard-earned reputation, while they were still regarded as upstarts by those who thought punk should've stopped in 1984. Very few had done as much as Rancid to bridge the gap between the generations. The band's enthusiastic championing of punk old and new was beyond reproach. Though Rancid's own records were becoming less frequent, the years between saw the band members actively supporting the network in one form or another.

Inevitably, the band toured extensively following the 2009 release of *Dominoes*. This placed new challenges on the band's family men: Matt and Lars. Lars told *Louder Than War* in 2012: 'I know there have been many challenges, but I can't really think of one that stands out. I'm sure we all have personal ones, and for me these days it's leaving the kids to go on tour'.

The shows were memorable, and many were immortalised in the form of digital downloads of 37 shows spread between 2006 and 2008. These are covered later in the book.

Between 2009 and 2014, much of the band members' time was spent on side projects. Devils Brigade finally got around to releasing their eponymous debut album in 2010: the lineup including Tim on guitar and DJ Bonebrake on drums. The album was basically psychobilly, with Matt singing and playing upright bass. He also guested on an album by Tiger Army during Rancid's downtime.

Meanwhile, Lars put together a crack Oi! outfit called The Old Firm Casuals, with Casey Watson and Paul Rivas from Never Healed, and Gabriel Gavriloff. The Old Firm Casuals' sound was what Lars had wanted for The Bastards at the start of the decade. The Casuals issued a series of 45s with the likes of Last Resort between 2011 and 2014. Check out 'Army Of One'. Their debut album *This Means War* came out on Oi The Boat Records and the German label Randale in 2014. The band gigged the world over, especially in Europe, where they memorably played the Rebellion Festival in Blackpool, England. Lars Oi! peers soon christened him The Guv'nor – bet he loved that.

Tim started using the moniker Tim Timebomb during this period. No Tim Armstrong solo records surfaced, but his output as a record producer and as part of his Tim Timebomb and Friends consortium was prolific to say the least. Over 30 tracks were released: digitally, and in many cases on 7" vinyl. Covers recorded include 'Concrete Jungle', 'Brown Eyed Girl', 'Summer Of '69', and past Rancid classics ('It's Quite Alright'). There were also self-penned songs such as 'She's Drunk All The Time', which appeared on his album *Special Lunacy*: released in 2013 on Pirate Press Records.

One of Tim's friends was Kevin Bivona: a member of The Interrupters. They were Tim's proteges, their career getting off the ground during this period, helped by Tim's song 'Family'. He also produced and worked on the band's self-titled debut album. Furthermore, Tim Timebomb's *RockNRoll Theater* TV show was premiered in 2011 on VEVO. Starring both Tim and Lars, it is absolute joy, with great performances from Lars and Tim, with Lars clearly loving every second as the baddie. The punk musical material is worth checking too. Tim told the *Epitaph* website in 2011: 'Doing a show centred on musical theatre, isn't really a stretch for me. For 25 years I've been making music and collaborating with friends, been involved in hundreds of videos, and it's really just an extension of my world'.

An album pulling together much of the work by Tim Timebomb and Friends and *RockNRoll Theater* was issued on Hellcat as download-only in 2012. It was titled *Tim Timebomb Sings Songs From RockNRoll Theater*.

Another of Tim's projects during Rancid's hiatus was with Jimmy Cliff. Tim produced and collaborated on the reggae star's magnificent 2012 album *Rebirth*. It included covers of The Clash's 'Guns Of Brixton' and Rancid's 'Ruby Soho'. The LP went on to win a Grammy for both Jimmy and Tim, and is a real highlight of Tim's career, in my opinion.

As if this wasn't enough, in 2013, Epitaph released Transplants' third – and to date, final – album *In A Warzone*.

A lot for any band to cram into their vacation, I'm sure you'll agree. But in 2013, Rancid got together to start work on their eighth album. In all, it took a year to create, but the process was simple. Just two Los Angeles studios – The Boat and Red Star – were used to record the material for ...*Honor Is All We Know*: which from now on will be termed *Honor*. A minimal amount of guests were used. Skinhead Rob Aston, Brett Gurewitz, Mick McColgan and Big Chris Hollosy helped on backing vocals. Big Chris also helped with a spirited series of handclaps. Kevin Bivona provided Hammond organ and piano. That's it. This basic working setup, contributed to the album's sound. Much to the joy of diehards, there was a return to raw, raucous punk rock and gritty reggae, and the latter point was crucial: Rancid doing their version of reggae. Some of the *Dominoes* deep cuts were reggae alright, but not obviously Rancid. Dub techniques and bombastic Studio One-sounding brass sounded great, but the sound of distorted guitar and passionate vocals over a punchy backbeat were what we were after. On *Honor*'s fourth cut 'Evil's My Friend', we got exactly that, but only after a healthy dose of frenetic high-octane punk – not as hardcore as on either of the self-titled records, but not as accessible as *Indestructible* either. It was the sound of Rancid playing Rancid.

The critics thought so too. *The L.A. Times* said exactly this in 2014, while briefly running through some pointers of the band's 23-year career: 'They've been Bay Area gutter punks, unlikely mainstream rock starts, reggae revival champions and L.A. pop producers. Now the four guys in Rancid are back where they started: making three-minute shards of scuzzy but ultimately warm-hearted punk rock'. The warm-hearted point is interesting – the messages of unity; the empathy with people who struggle; the support for populations across the globe; the sentimental personal lyrics. Warm-hearted is correct.

The album cover harked back to a previous album's sleeve. The phrase '… Honor Is All We Know' was scratched out on the cover, like Tim's scrawl of the album title on the *Wolves* cover. The logo was obviously in place, and the sleeve art featured Rancid's tools of the trade: a Gibson SG, Gretsch hollow body, a Fender Precision bass, with Branden's bass drum and Doc Martens. The front cover shot was by J. Bonner, the back one by Ryan Foltz of Dropkick Murphys. The inside-cover photograph was by Judd Sherman and was a bird's-eye view of Tim and Matt looking out from a stage edge, over a sweaty, packed crowd.

Rancid wrote all songs except for the title track which was by Tim. That song was also among those recorded by Tim Timebomb and Friends. Competition, then!!

'Back Where I Belong' (Rancid)

Never a more apt title. A rip-roaring opener. It's as if the band couldn't wait to get back to doing what they do best: playing songs like this. The anticipation levels are through the roof as Lars bellows the words immediately before the chorus. And of course, it has a huge, huge chorus.

> Well, you won't see us coming cos we're already gone
> I'm Back, I'm back, I'm back to where I belong
> I've been gone away for too long and I'm back to where I belong

This song has that favourite Rancid theme, of unity. Unity comes with doing what we know and love. There is little more unifying than that. Back where we belong.

A word about Branden Steineckert's performance. It's staggering. His pattern is simple enough to provide the backbone, but the fills, crashes and rolls really lift the cut. It's exhilarating, especially when you factor in the light-fingered fluency of Matt's bass line. Richly distorted guitars work with the vocal exchanges, and the whole thing fizzes.

'Raise Your Fist' (Rancid)

Defiance. Unity. Belief. Bravery. Solidarity. Does anyone ever tire of songs with these themes? Thought not. A song with such a title, must have these themes. The lyric is a call to arms, and though the words appear non-specific, there's a hint of working-peoples' rights, waking up and not accepting a sanitised way of life

Apathetic revolution, people get put to sleep,
As the people wake up they'll be rioting in the streets

The power of the people is underrated in modern life (still), and the chorus is a dose of belief and the potency of such strength.

Raise Your Fist! Against the power!
Oppress the power that exists!

Tim's gravelly and super-slurred voice is an accentuating characteristic as the years pass. The straightforward D/G/C chord structure works well on this number.

'Collision Course' (Rancid)

This was the first promo taken from the album, and together with 'Evil's My Friend' and 'Honor Is All We Know', featured on a video issued as an album taster. It was a black-and-white film with no thrills; the band performing the three tunes.

It's high-octane, raucous stuff over another elementary sequence (D/C/F/G). The lyric is very much aimed at the heart of the 1970s' first-generation punk fans and the folk who signed up soon after. It mentions vinyl records, punk discos and punk rock radio hidden away on frequencies well away from the mainstream. Many tuned in to the punk and reggae sounds played by the likes of John Peel on England's Radio 1: where Steel Pulse were played alongside The Undertones. The aforementioned Don Letts spun reggae tunes at The Roxy. Punk and reggae became inextricably linked, very quickly. The work of those early DJs playing those records was critical, opening a worldwide audience. Tim noticed this across the Atlantic. And Rancid, of course, went on to strengthen this link further, especially on *Life*.

The emphasis is on the punk/reggae union. UK street punkers Sham 69 are name-checked in the first verse: 'Sham 69, roots reggae on my table/With a 45 record too, on the turntable'. Lars and Tim share vocal duties – the interchange between the latter's slurred gritty soul and the former's clear grainy passion, again working superbly. The lyric is sentimental, and this is easily overlooked amidst the track's bombastic ram-raid feel. Many of you would've had that radio tuned, had the station-light glow, and would've heard that sound of your needle hitting the record.

> Well, the glow of the light on my radio dial
> For better beats from the record file
> I dropped the needle watching the cretins hop
> While I'm playing Pac-man at the record shop

'Evil's My Friend' (Rancid)
The album's third promo single, and many say is the album's best track. The groove is nippy, with a wicked distorted guitar riffing razor-sharp over it. It's made for dancing to in a dark, steamy punk club with a bottle of Newcastle Brown or a can of Red Stripe in your hand. It's Rancid playing their version of Jamaican music. This point is significant. It's as fast as ska, but with a deep boss reggae snatch which stops it from running away. Tim's voice is perfectly matched to the sonic – an instrument in itself, rhythmically snapping out the words, slotting them in beside Hammond-organ flashes. The Interrupters' Kevin Bivona really shows his style. Strong reggae tunes are often all-the-better for organ washes. There's no Vic Rugierro on this album.

And the track does indeed sound evil. It's wicked, sinister and effecting. It matches the lyric: about how evil can drag you down into the ground. You must fight it. The song suggests a street/urban/criminal evil, but obviously, it can apply to legal, authoritative evil that bangs away at society and its liberty: 'If you wanna go and get 'em, you better stand and fight/You're never gonna let 'em take away your right'.

'Honor Is All We Know' (Tim Timebomb)
Rancid often bunched a clutch of singles together on their albums. And here, three follow each other. Tim wrote the title track alone, and a version was recorded without the rest of the band for his Tim Timebomb and Friends project. A loud, proud number, its Celtic vibe resembles the work of the band's long-time Boston friends and labelmates Dropkick Murphys. There are no whistles or pipes though.

Each lead vocalist takes a turn on a verse. Tim starts off, Matt does a resonant turn on verse two and Lars – as he often does – almost steals the show with his verse coming packed with personality as ever. Each turn is followed by a melodic guitar run over the verse chords – each slightly different, ranging from delicious guitar versions of the vocal melody to rock-'n'-roll runs and gritty riffage. It all creates a big track.

The song divides a few though. Some – like *Consequence Of Sound* in 2014 – mentioned 'the by-numbers pop punk riffs bookending the vacuous vocals'. Others were more favourable. In the same year, *Punk News* praised

'Armstrong, Freeman and Frederiksen each taking a turn at the vocals as they urge solidarity, forgiveness and respect to their listeners'.

The lyrics are generic and can be applied to many walks of life. Good art is open to interpretation.

> It takes courage to make it in this land
> So don't forget, but forgive every man
> And prosperity's river, it will forever flow
> Honor is among us, honor is all we know

Whatever your view, this song cannot be ignored. Whilst it doesn't break new ground, it is powerful, and proudly pins the band's colours well-and-truly to the mast of brotherhood, unity and punk rock.

'A Power Inside' (Rancid)

A song tandem to 'Raise Your Fist', this time focussing on unions and the power of workers, rather than blindly oppressing the employers' power being forced upon them. So, a different take on power. The solidarity, support and defiance of a good union, gives the workers power in its ranks. The power is not just with the unions though – every worker has a fire inside us that can be kindled to make change, to better him or herself. So, it's like a chain of power. Unions are great as representative bodies, but workers have power inside themselves: 'There's a power in a union, there's a power inside/There's a power inside every man alive'. Tim's fixation on working-class rights has constantly arisen in Rancid's work: 'Union Blood', 'Harry Bridges', and now 'A Power Inside'.

The song itself has a protest-song feel, encouraging every member to stand up and sing with pride, to believe in every syllable. It has a rabble-rousing quality, augmented by the Oi! mob feel. Add how the riff sounds similar to The Clash's 'White Riot', and you have a banger. Make sure your subscriptions are up to date, people.

'In The Streets' (Rancid)

This marks a slight change on the album. Firstly, it sets off a series of tracks where the lead vocals are split 50/50 – Tim by and large having taken the lead vocals thus far. Secondly, a little more variety surfaces across the tracks.

This is slower in tempo, but nevertheless is the album's best street-punk anthem. The terrace-chant chorus is the killer. Moving with the A/D chord changes, it has a more-reflective tint that differentiates it from the other songs. It's also one of Tim and Lars' best interchanging vocals.

It's the album's one personal lyric: I suspect, anyway. The central character is Kristine – a girl living on the street, full to the max with life, despite her situation. The lyric comes from someone who obviously knew street life – the darkness, the filth, the blight of it. But the impression I get here is of a young woman who called the street *home*, and gave it the best she could, knowing her world would someday come to an end.

> Kristine with the wild grin
> In the future with the world to end
> You'll leave my heart broken then
> One thousand times again

Her wild grin could've been the result of a substance, of course. Scrutinising the final line, it's possible that Tim would've liked to be closer to Kristine or became frustrated with her.

'Face Up' (Rancid)

'Face Up' is light on its feet, with a whipping guitar riff in C major, kicking the track straight into gear. There's no hanging about before the first verse nor the chanted chorus. It has a barroom party feel, and is the album's shortest cut, at just over 90 seconds in length.

Lyrically there's a personal theme. It's humble, despite the violence of Lars' opening lines. The protagonist has gratitude for music taking him away from alcohol, bars and trouble, and to a new life. Music as salvation. The song is a further sequel to 'Radio'.

> Well, it's just another day of getting into trouble
> Chasing all the booze with another bottle
> And towards live music and bands
> When I hit that summer with an angel on my shoulder
> Another day living, another day older
> Thank God I made it this far
> Tell my story to the boys with a guitar

Short, snappy, redemptive and succinct stuff.

'Already Dead' (Rancid)

Another split vocal track, another shift in feel. The simple A/D chord structure underpins a change in mood allowing the dark and sinister tone to match the lyric's theme.

'Already Dead' was one of half a dozen tracks drip-fed to listeners online prior to *Honor*'s October 2014 release. The song was received to universal acclaim, more so than any other track on the album. Stereogum called it, 'the latest song that they've shared, and is the best one we've heard yet'.

It's a good example of the band's craft. It sounds like a traditional folk song: the kind sung by the poor, lamenting their struggle. But by adding plenty of urban street grit and street-punk swagger to the high-octane tempo, Rancid made 'Already Dead' a strong punk number. Lars comes over as the young hustler, his voice full of vibrancy and energy but fascinated by the dark side. Tim's slur makes him appear much older, and wiser than Lars (he does have some ten years on him anyway), and he delivers his lines with the weariness of experience, hinting at the danger.

The muddy, dirty spaghetti-western flavour of a song like 'Django' is also present – the imagery of these cowboy films; splattered brains blown out by a Colt 45, the victim lying facedown in a puddle. Tim's character is dead inside after the life he's had, yet he lives on purely in physical form. 'Well, I've been to hell and back one million times'. The outcome is he doesn't care about his actions, so cross him at your peril. 'See, I lie, cheat and steal, and I'll break your fucking neck/And you'll curse out my name when you take your last breath'. Lars' character listens, taking note.

'Diabolical' (Rancid)

This is a catchy chorus you'll have in your head for hours, having heard it just once. The split vocal is one of the reasons it works so well: Lars's bright clarity; Tim's slurred depth. The track is one of the album's most accessible, with a big chorus and bright distorted guitars. The bright, poppy melody is juxtaposed against the lyric. The verse storytelling introduces us to new characters Andy, Melanie and Penny. I'm not sure if they're real people or just characters from Tim's imagination. I like the way the lyric portrays disagreements getting out of hand and then becoming violent. At this point, an allegory is made between violence and a dance, hence the chorus' dance metaphor.

> One man gives an opinion
> Another man takes offence
> When it comes to violence
> It's a diabolical dance

'Diabolical' was one of the tracks the band drip-fed prior to the album's release. It's also a song that would've been very much at home on *Wolves*.

'Malfunction' (Rancid)

The feel here is retro, not retro punk this time. Occasionally, Rancid songs have a Pete Townshend influence: notably in the staccato chord riffs. Branden's pounding drum pattern, supported by tambourine and handclaps, is quintessential 1960s. The Faces are another band that spring to mind. This all gets turbocharged of course. The distorted six-string work is present – no attempt was made to obtain a jangly Rickenbacker sound, for example. There's a tasty guitar solo in the outro too.

It's a decent track, and the varying feel stops *Honor* from being a pure shouty street-punk record – no bad thing, but nowhere near as wide-ranging as *Life*.

'Now We're Through With You' (Rancid)

This is full of energy and is the nearest thing on *Honor* to the material on either of the self-titled albums, by a mile. Brett Gurewitz's production is cleaner and glossier. But the gutsy, blistering pace reminds us that this is a punk rock band. It's fast and furious, and Matt's bass speeds along like greased lightning. Tim's vocal is indecipherable at times, his now-deeper slur a throwback to the band's earlier work.

The lyric theme is straightforward – about turning your back on somebody who's wronged you. There is a gang feel, of sticking up for your brethren: 'You took blood from the wrong crew/Now we're through with you'. The words are not specific, giving no clue to whom they're aimed at. It could be, picking a fight with the wrong people – like The Distillers did around the time Tim and Brody split – or street gang squabbles. It's open to interpretation. Many of the *Honor* lyrics are like this: generic rather than specific.

'Everybody's Sufferin'' (Rancid)

A highlight of the record, and another shift in musical emphasis, but to an area well inside Rancid's sphere: ska. Rather than the grittier tone of 'Evil's My Friend', 'Everybody's Sufferin'' has an obvious sharp 2 Tone quality with its The Selector-style groove. It harks back to their classic 'Too Much Pressure', with the lyric repetitions supplementing a rock-solid groove. You can really lose yourself dancing to this, and you can visualise the steam and sweat running down the walls of a club. Kevin Bivona's organ-playing stands out, marking him as a future star: something that came to fruition with the emergence of The Interrupters shortly after.

The limited lyrical content focusses on the struggles of populations in times of economic and sociological depression: 'Everywhere you're going, people they all suffer ... Everybody's sufferin', across this land'.

A final example of the variety of the album's second half and its excellent sequencing.

'Grave Digger' (Rancid)

Honor closes with a thumping right hook of street punk. 'Grave Digger' is a blitz attack, with a rapid-fire tempo and a full-on wall-of-sound juggernaut backing. The verse vocals are split between Tim and Lars, before the whiplash chorus arrives.

The lyric savages those born into wealth who exploit those poorer than them. So, they exploit most of us, then. They dig society's grave as a result. Tim's writing has real vitriol when certain subjects take centre stage. This anger could've worked on their debut record, alongside urban blight and other examples of inequality. In attacking the gravedigger, Rancid support those regular people who suffer at the grave digger's expense.

Well, you prey on the weak who are trying to survive
You jump on the backbone that's keeping you alive

Contemporary Releases

Honor saw a series of promo single releases to help market the album release. By-and-large these were digital files, but CD promos were issued in some countries. None of these made the *Billboard* or UK singles charts.

'Collision Course' (Rancid)
Release date: 30 September 2014
CD promo issued in Australia only.

'Honor Is All We Know' (Tim Timebomb)
Release date: 2014
CD promo single issued in Europe.

'Evil's My Friend' (Rancid)
Release date: 30 September 2014
Download only.

'Face Up' (Rancid)
Release date: 7 October 2014
Download only.

'Already Dead' (Rancid)
Release date: 14 October 2014
Download.

'Diabolical' (Rancid)
Release date: 21 October 2014
Download.

...Honor Is All We Know (Expanded edition) (2015)
This was released on vinyl and CD and had three bonus cuts. Not all were included on all pressings however, so check before you buy. Both sides of the stand-alone 2014 single 'Turn In Your Badge' b/w 'Something To Believe In A World Gone Mad' were included. For details of these tracks, see 'Stand-alone Singles' later in the book.

'Breakdown' (Rancid)
A ska banger. An instant snappy chorus and tight, close country-esque guitar, set the track. There are nice Hammond flashes from Kevin Bivona, with a solid mid-tempo pace and Lars and Tim singing the verses, respectively. Maybe it was left off the album because it's quite similar to 'Everybody's Sufferin'' with its rock-solid Selector/2-Tone groove.

'Rancid's Barmy Army'

This fourth bonus cut was included on the Japanese expanded edition. Tim takes the lead on 61 seconds of fast punk guts, reminiscent of Motorhead's 'R-A-M-O-N-E-S'. The band name is spelt out in the chorus, see: 'Barmy Army!/R-A-N-C-I-D!'.

Trouble Maker (LP) (2017)

Personnel:
Tim Timebomb, Lars Frederiksen: guitar, vocals
Matt Freeman: bass, vocals
Branden Steineckert: drums
Label: Hellcat
Producer: Brett Gurewitz
Release date: 9 June 2017
Chart positions: US: 23, UK: 57
Running time: 35:44

Three years passed between *Honor* and *Trouble Maker:* Rancid's ninth and – at the time of writing – most recent LP. A reason for the quicker turnaround was, apparently, Brett Gurewitz's suggestion that three songs in pre-production for the second Tim Armstrong solo album were in fact more suited to a new Rancid album. The band originally were going to schedule an interim EP in late 2015, but this was canned when they decided to go with Gurewitz's idea.

There was an official 2015 Rancid release, however. A second compilation *All The Moon Stompers* was issued on Randale Records: a popular collection which will be covered later.

Tim Timebomb and Friends remained busy during the intervening period, and The Old Firm Casuals released *A Butcher's Banquet* in 2016. There was nothing new from Devil's Brigade.

Interestingly, the *Trouble Maker* sleeve saw the return of the original handstamp-effect logo used on the band's debut album. The front cover itself had the same red and black colour scheme as *Indestructible*, with a picture of the Brooklyn Bridge gracing the backdrop, with a lonely spiky-haired punk sitting strumming a guitar on the Brooklyn shore: quite evocative.

The album itself trod a similar path to *Honor*, with Rancid doing what they do best, slightly less Oi!-influenced, but still choc-full of gritty high-tempo punk-and-roll. Just one ska song was present, alongside stompers and punked-up retro stylings. However, it was a *touch* melancholy, giving rise to a folk-punk crossover feel. There wasn't much psychobilly, more's the pity. The album's 17 tracks were squeezed into under 37 minutes.

The lyric themes were reflective, especially on 'Telegraph Avenue'. Elsewhere they were again non-specific. The songwriting credits were different again. This time, Tim wrote several songs on his own: credited to Tim Timebomb. Elsewhere, whole group credits were made by listing individual names.

As with *Honor*, several tracks were leaked online. The videos were filmed in the band's now-infamous garage. Reviews were mixed. *Trouble Maker* seemed to suffer, as critics rounded on Rancid seeming content to stick to what they did best. *Punk News* once more led the way in 2017, saying, 'Admittedly, there isn't a single bad song on *Trouble Maker*. The problem is, there also isn't a single song on it that shows that they've grown in 26 years'. *Wall Of Sound* claimed, '*Trouble Maker* isn't a bad album, but I'd struggle to call it a good one'. Some reviews were good. *Pitchfork* concluded *Trouble Maker* to be 'far and wide their strongest effort since 2000's self-titled'.

The spirit of punk is doing exactly what you want. Some – often the music press – mistake this as the need to do something *different*. It doesn't have to be this way. Early in their career, Rancid did so much more than most to mix up punk, hip hop, rockabilly, ska, dub, reggae and hardcore. And a *Billboard* placing of 23 indicated fans were happy.

The 2017 punk scene saw a whole host of new bands make their presence felt, such as Idles. Metal – especially melodic progressive metal – continued to fuse with punk. The presence of heavy metal in punk was nothing new of course. The new wave of heavy metal in the UK, directly influenced the likes of Discharge and GBH back in the early-1980s. On 'Killing Zone' in 2003, Rancid had drawn the two genres together.

By now, peers such as New Found Glory and Dropkick Murphys had huge fan bases, and easily rode any critical wave. The same, of course, applied to Rancid. The band might push boundaries again someday, but in 2017 they served up an album with a 10-per cent-or-so tweak. *Trouble Maker* saw the band doing what they know, crafted in a reflective – rather than bombastic – way. Fine by me.

'Track Fast' (Timebomb, Freeman, Frederiksen, Steineckert)
Another whirlwind of an opener, and it's over and out in 67 seconds. The riff is Motorhead-esque – a kind of dirty metal-punk hybrid, like, err... Rancid meets Motorhead! Only two chords needed: G and F.

All three singers, feature. The question-and-answer verse features Matt and Tim. Tim's voice had matured – or maybe that should be, weathered – over the years: so-much-so that the two were getting closer sonically at this point. Tim's slur and grit and Matt's bear growl will always be distinct, however. Lars and Tim alternate on the chorus: 'Track fast (track fast)/Track fast (track fast)/It's all too fast'.

'Ghost Of A Chance' (Timebomb)
Another short one, and the album's first promo single. Tim's vocal is quite something. His voice, as I said previously, had weathered. The gritty soulful slur is part-pirate/part-barroom troubadour. This accentuates the reflective feel. The lyric has a simple theme: *Most think we get one shot at making life better*. So, recognise this, at least. It's up to you.

Well, these walls are high enough to keep you locked in
Locked in for a lifetime
Well, you're one lousy step from not making it
You only got a ghost of a chance, my brother
You only got a ghost of a chance

The emphasised slur on 'my brother' is sublime.

The song is over after merely 95 seconds. The rhythm section is so quick, it's almost like a madcap bluegrass number – something that underpins Tim's weathered growl perfectly, as it goes. There's blistering guitar work from Lars, full of up-front solo work.

The track's video showed the band playing in their garage. Subtitles were splashed across the screen, showing the lyrics. Tim's vocal style – despite being indecipherable on occasion – doesn't necessitate this. It's nothing like the singing on the band's debut, which in comparison was virtually impossible to comprehend.

'Telegraph Avenue' (Timebomb)

Folk punk. A sombre, reflective, commemorative number, recounting the days in 1969 when all eyes were on Telegraph Avenue, Berkeley. The avenue is adjacent to People's Park and stretches to Oakland: Tim and Matt's home turf, of course. In 1969, People's Park was the location for free speech and anti-Vietnam War demonstrations, with the National Guard being called in to apply state control. One man – James Rector – was shot dead as he sat on a roof above Telegraph Avenue as police fired random shots to quell protests. Tear gas canisters were fired as police chased protestors. Ronald Reagan was the Californian Governor at the time.

The song honours the rebellious spirit of the era and of this location. Verse one takes us to the Telegraph Avenue that Tim knew as a teenager, playing music and hanging out:

When I was only 17
I knew what I had to do
So I grabbed my left-handed guitar
And I headed out to Telegraph Avenue.

The second and third verses then move to the demonstrations:

Governor Reagan had enough
So the National Guard they pushed on through
Tear gas and riot police on Telegraph Avenue

The song comes to an end with Tim dedicating it to the memories of those who stood for free speech:

The ones who stand for freedom of speech
This one goes out to you
Well I can still hear your voice on Telegraph Avenue

The album's second single, the video again featured the band playing the song in their garage. It drew some of the fiercest criticism when it was released. *Wall*

Of Sound scribe Dave Mullins stated, 'Telegraph Avenue is not just an album low-point, it might just be the worst song Rancid have ever put out'. He is entitled to his opinion, I guess.

The song has a mournful quality, helped by the A-minor key: appropriate, given the subject matter. Telegraph Avenue is close to the very heart of Rancid, geographically, demographically and historically. Throw in its demonstration history and the legacy, and you have a song that articulates this respectfully. The 'na-na-na''s in the chorus are almost ghost-like.

'An Intimate Close-Up of a Street Punk Trouble Maker'
(Timebomb)

Dave Mullins does acknowledge that the record's fourth and fifth tracks are 'easily two of the best songs on the album (especially where Armstrong's vocals are concerned)'. Funny that: Lars takes much of the lead vocal on 'Where I'm Going'.

'An Intimate Close-Up Of A Street Punk Trouble Maker' is easily Rancid's longest song title by some distance. Another wonderful melodic single-string guitar hook gets the track going. It's one of the best latter-day Rancid numbers in terms of craft. It is quick: real quick. Branden pounds out the lightning drum pattern with Matt's Dee Dee-style bass, locked in. The guitar melody flies in and out, with Tim's voice resonant and soulful. The background vocals are simply fantastic; the cries of 'Trouble Maker', potent. It has textures, but they are not provided by clever production techniques or multitracking. It's in the track's construction, using two guitars, four vocalists and an amazing rhythm section to the max.

The subject is the world seen through the eyes of a busker, playing tunes, getting passers-by to leave a coin if they like. The world refuses the people liberty, often by birthright, so for some, busking is the last bastion. The busking metaphor can be applied to many others stuck on the lower rungs of life's ladder. They can only express themself properly this way.

Trouble maker, you got nothing to lose
Trouble maker, busking at the station
Trouble maker, yeah we're being refused
Trouble maker, refused by creation

'Where I'm Going' (Timebomb, Freeman, Frederiksen, Steineckert)

This is the album's one ska number. Lars takes most of the lead vocal, but Tim sings too. Lars sings his lines with full-on character. Take the song's first verse for instance, which has nice variations in tone and emphasis; bright and piercing. This track was one of the handful leaked prior to the album's release. It was also the most universally well received. *Rolling Stone* referred to its 'rocksteady vamp of light guitar chords and organ plunks'.

'Where I'm Going' has a stomping ska rhythm, and is a dance floor filler. It's ska and reggae more than rocksteady: which is slower in tempo than both its predecessor (ska) and successor (reggae). Its boisterous strutting groove is laid down as tightly as possible by the dream team of Branden and Matt – Branden's snare drum punctuating the verse and chorus finales brilliantly. The aforementioned licks and tricks from guitars and organ, add the colour. The lyrics tell a tale of not giving fucks. The protagonist's selfish behaviour goes to the extent of smashing things up and causing annihilation: all fuelled by booze. It really can take you on a road to hell.

Retaliation is my crime
Communication, a waste of time
Inebriation suits me fine
Incarcerate my own mind

The keyboard-playing is courtesy of Kevin Bivona.

'Buddy' (Timebomb)
The folk punk feel of the album is present on 'Buddy'. Mournful lyric? Check. Storytelling? Check. Weathered lead vocal? Check. Simple D/G/A chords? Check. And... Bob Dylan-style harmonica? Check. Well, kind of. Actually, it's Kevin Bivona on an accordion. But there are enough classic Rancid touches (Lars's single-string guitar melody; the gritty backing track) to keep it from going too far in the folk direction. And it's played at breakneck speed.

This is a nostalgic, personal lyric about friendship, and an ode to one departed from this earth. It's heartfelt stuff, recounting days gone by, of BART train rides into San Francisco. There's a clear message here to make the most of our time on Earth. Again, Tim's weathered vocal enhances the words and provides depth. It's one of the album's most resonant tracks.

'Farewell Lola Blue' (Timebomb)
Another resonant track, this time with an historical focus on the Battle Of Corregidor, where Japan completed the conquest of the Philippines during World War Two. American fighter pilots took part in the campaign, and the losses were considerable. This song deals with one such pilot. It's a poignant anthem. No name is given, but the mystery dive bomber pilot went down in the battle, and the name Lola Blue was painted on the side of his aircraft.

May 6, 1942, now was a good year to be 22
To have a cause and something to fight for
And be in love with Lola Blue

Heart-breaking, eh? Rancid can produce a tune like this, with strong, meaningful lyrics that educate as well as entertain. The song has a huge chorus,

125

wonderful lyrics, and is inevitably well-crafted. There's light and shade, tension in the build prior to the chorus that adds to the feel, and a great, passionate Lars vocal. And it fades out at the end: unusual for Rancid!! Their tracks usually come to a tight stop.

How many kids looked up what happened over the Coral Sea off the Philippines on 6 May, 1942? Quite a few, I bet. I did.

'All American Neighbourhood' (Timebomb, Freeman, Frederiksen, Steineckert)

Pulsating stuff. This is the album's closest thing to the band's debut work – full-throttle backing, nasty aggressive guitars, sirens, and an overall uneasy and sinister sonic. This matches the lyric, which paints a picture of a nation that's going to the dogs. It's now riddled with lowlife criminals exploiting everyday people, both legally and illegally; doctors and pharmacists on the make, pushing drugs. They are dealers too, see. Legitimate? Maybe. The authorities don't mind: they're probably in on it:

> Drug dealer pharmacist, have 'em all
> Hand out prescriptions for more than all
> Once upon a time this town was drug free
> Now it's ruled by Oxy

'Bovver Rock and Roll' (Timebomb, Freeman, Frederiksen, Steineckert)

Another single from the album, and at the time of writing, the last Rancid single to make the *Billboard* chart. It was well-received by critics too.

Like on *Honor*, Rancid take a retro music styling, and do their own thing with it. The obvious comparison here is with The Rolling Stones. The Keith Richard-style riff, strutting groove and shouty lyrics, are all certainly characteristics consistent with the Stones' *Exile On Main Street* era. However, I feel it has more in common with British glam rock; Keith's guitar was rarely this fat and distorted. British glam had this sound, coupled with the loud pounding drums and strutting rhythm. 'Bovver Rock and Roll' does all this, with Chuck Berry rock-'n'-roll guitar soloing, crafted backing vocals and Tim's snarled singing.

The song is about being a young punk. We like our music, and we like our fashion, particularly when it comes to the footwear. Bovver boots was a common term used for *Dr. Martens* boots: that staple wardrobe item of punk rockers, moon stompers and skinheads. So it makes sense to write a stomping, kicking song celebrating this, and perform it with swagger.

And that's exactly what Rancid do. The song is set in the early-1970s, when bovver boots were finding their way into those wardrobes. It's a kind of history lesson again, citing the lying Richard Nixon and the troubles in Cambodia. It takes us through the hippy years to the late-1970s. To forget and escape the woes of the outside world, young skinheads – and later, punks – got together on a Saturday night, and danced:

Rock and roll need an 8-track tape
Peace and love now war hate
Sun's coming up now, we did alright
Let's do it again next Saturday night

'Make It Out Alive' (Timebomb, Freeman, Frederiksen, Steineckert)

One of the album's standouts. The brotherhood of life in the military has an ally in the brotherhood shared within the Rancid ranks. Remember: friendship first, band second. The song isn't about Rancid though. Military life was used as a theme on several *Dominoes* songs. The lyric describes scenarios only military families like Tim's could envisage.

I drank water from a bloody creek
The only life I could find
I lost my leg in the wilderness
And the fire made me blind

The atrocities of war can't really be comprehended unless you experience them. This song – despite the vibrant tempo and another huge chorus – is almost a lament. It speaks of suffering and pain caused to those affected throughout history: all in the name of the United States: 'Mr Lincoln, I have served you proud'. Of course, many soldiers across a great many wars, did not return.

Another word about Branden's drumming. The rolling, attacking drum rhythm drives the song on like a military sortie. How can you fail to produce good material with a chassis such as this?

'Molly Make Up Your Mind' (Timebomb)

Blink and you'll miss it – even with a key change at the song's finale. This obviously Celtic-flavoured ditty runs for 81 seconds. The chorus is repeated over and over. It's gang-like, with simple chords (A/D/A/E) and a sea-shanty feel: which – along with Tim's hoary lead vocal – suit it down to the ground.

This folk-punk fable is about a girl (Molly) who refuses to lay down roots and leaves a trail of debris behind. A deal is then done, and she runs off with the cash. Molly is one step ahead of the rest.

Molly obtained certain information
Zero by zero is zero equation
Got that money as she left that place

127

'I Got Them Blues Again' (Timebomb)

Another folk-punk lament, with mournful lyrics about being down on your luck: the blues, in other words. There's a lot of craft in this recording. Big backing vocals, for instance. If I'm honest, it has a little too much crammed in (in my view) and is one of the few times the craft hijacks the song itself. We're not talking progressive rock, but a simpler version would've done fine for me.

The lyric references lost love and the lost identity of an area: in this case, Tim and Matt's neighbourhood around Telegraph Avenue. The faceless moneymen who've exploited Berkeley and Oakland, are targeted.

The sequencing of the album allows a blues lament, a Celtic fable and a song about the tragedy and horror of war, to follow each other.

'Beauty Of the Pool Hall' (Timebomb)

This is the nearest thing to rockabilly on the album, with a combination of guitars and a pummelling, snappy backbeat. The fact a pool hall is the setting, adds to the 1950s flavour. The whole thing has a ragged, raucous feel that harks back to the band's classic *Wolves* period. Tim's vocal is fantastic, portraying a genuine working-class ethic, revelling in pool-hall lifestyle, and raising a glass to the inhabitants. However, the lyrics are again a lament. The main character regularly visits the hall, but is homeless, living in a cardboard box. She is kind but takes no shit. Eventually, she disappears, never to be seen again. It's set in San Francisco, with Union Square and North Beach mentioned.

'Say Goodbye to Our Heroes' (Timebomb, Freeman, Frederiksen, Steineckert)

Folk gives way to punk rock for the final quartet of songs. This song pays homage to the heroes of punk rock who passed away too soon, and it's played in passionate, heartfelt fashion. Tim's vocal is emotional, wandering in and out of tune: something that adds to the feeling. Punk rock is something he believes in, and his fervour comes over. The song has a pumped-up energy, strong tempo and excitement. There's a brief speech clarifying the purpose behind the song, though it's not really needed: the words do the job just fine.

Spoken song sections are an interesting point on *Trouble Maker*, and on *Honor*: or, the lack of them. The ubiquitous rapping that at times plagued *Dominoes,* doesn't feature here at all. Maybe that and the Transplants albums, exhausted it.

The respect given to punk rock and its legends, shone through on many occasions on Rancid records – 'Collision Course' from the last album; 'Wrongful Suspicion' from *Life*; 'Radio' from *Let's Go*. This time it focuses on those who left this earth too early: 'This song goes out to our punk rock heroes/You see, the flame that burns twice as bright, runs half as long'.

'I Kept a Promise' (Timebomb)

This is a thumping track, with a Vibrators influence – in my view – with its fat, chunky chorus and fists-aloft shouts of the song title. It's one of the album's longer tracks, checking in at just over three minutes. It's a personal lyric, detailing a post-gig episode at Parrington Hall, Seattle. This was between a young man and an elder, about the gift of music and how it makes things right. That day, the youngster made a vow to the cause of music, and to stay away from the things that may drag him down:

If he's given the gift of music, he should make the most of it
That music is a gift and it's everything that's right
I promise that I'll always keep it in my sights

One highlight is Lars' riffy guitar solo towards the song's coda.

I love the vision of an old punk passing on wisdom to the youngster, while sitting backstage looking out over the rooftops. Then the youngster wakes up the next day, thinks about what was said, and makes a pact. 26 years later, Tim made sure that promise was still being kept.

'Cold Cold Blood' (Timebomb, Freeman, Frederiksen, Steineckert)

This is probably my pick of the quartet of punk deep-cuts. Tim's voice stretches those chorus vowels over an E/A/E/B structure to spine-chilling effect. It's like a siren in places, melodic in others. It carries the melody, leads the arrangement, and opens the door for the backing vocals to respond. They are akin to military-parade chanting. The lyric is dark, about night-time killings and crimes. It's generic, and not specific to any one situation or episode, as far as I can tell.

The Motorhead influence is obvious: dirty solid punk rock-and-roll, shot out at speed.

'This Is Not The End' (Timebomb)

A clear message from the band to fans. We'll be back. Rancid signed off many of their albums with a line or a message to the Rancid nation. Take 'Golden Gate Fields' on *Rancid 5* for instance ('Til the next time'). This time, the communique is in the title, the message positive: 'Thinking every day, thinking every way/Keeping positive every single day'.

It's aggressive four-to-the-floor thrash punk. I feel for Branden's drum skins; they took such a thrashing during the 125 seconds of 'This Is Not The End'! Matt, of course, provides an express train of a bass line, crammed with finesse and technique. Gibson SG and hollow-body Gretsch guitars do the rest, sprawling out riffs, single note flurries and ringing chords. 'Got loyalty coming by the truckload'. A great way to sign off *Trouble Maker*. Its 36 minutes, flash by.

Contemporary Releases

The album's single releases followed the same format as did those from *Honor*. All were the same as the album recordings, and one – 'Bovver Rock and Roll' – did indeed make it into the *Billboard* chart.

'Where I'm Going' (Timebomb, Frederiksen, Freeman, Steineckert)
Release date: 2017
CD promo and download released in the US.

'Ghost Of a Chance' (Timebomb)
Release date: 2 May 2017
Download.

'Telegraph Avenue' (Timebomb)
Release date: 16 May 2017
Download.

'Farewell Lola Blue' (Timebomb)
Release date: 5 June 2017
Download.

'Say Goodbye To Our Heroes' (Timebomb, Frederiksen, Freeman, Steineckert)
Release date: 6 June 2017
Download.

'Bovver Rock And Roll' (Timebomb, Frederiksen, Freeman, Steineckert)
US Release date: 2017, Chart position: US: 26
Download, and the band's final *Billboard* single chart entry to date.

Trouble Maker (Expanded Edition) (2017)

This contained a 7" single featuring two unreleased tracks ('We Arrived On Time' and 'Go On And Rise Up'). See the stand-alone singles section for details. The expanded CD edition included the tracks tagged onto the end of the album.

Split Albums - BYO Split Series Volume 3 (Rancid and NOFX split LP, 2002)

Personnel:
Tim Armstrong, Lars Frederiksen: guitar, vocals
Matt Freeman: bass, guitar
Brett Reed: drums
Label: BYO
NOFX
Fat Mike: bass, vocals
Eric Melvin: guitar, vocals
El Hefe: guitar, trumpet, vocals
Erik Sandin: drums
Release Date: 5 March 2002
Chart position: Did not chart
Running time: 27·04

Better Youth Organisation (or BYO Records) – formed by Shawn and Mark Stem of Canadian punk band Youth Brigade – put out a series of split punk albums at the turn of the millennium. Each featured two contemporary punk bands. The releases were big news at the time, popular with fans and musicians alike. Bands involved included Leatherface, Hot Water Music, Swingin' Utters, Youth Brigade, Bouncing Souls, Anti-Flag, Alkaline Trio, One Man Army, NOFX and Rancid.

Apparently Tim approached NOFX about doing an album. The bands obviously went way back, Fat Wreck Chords issuing the *Radio Radio Radio* EP in 1993. Both bands are Californian, and both were produced by Brett Gurewitz. But stylistically, Rancid and NOFX have always been different. NOFX have always had a tongue-in-cheek sense of humour to their unique brand of breakneck punk rock. Rancid's gritty sound has always had a more traditional slant.

The release was eagerly anticipated. Reviews were favourable, with many scribes seemingly treating the whole thing as a competition to see who came out on top. In 2003, *Punk News* stated the release as being 'along the lines of 'Spiderman couldn't beat Batman' and so forth'.

The format was each band recording covers of the other band's material. This made for a bunch of interesting recordings. As this book is on Rancid, I'll give greater detail to their versions of NOFX tunes. But a quick overview of NOFX's interpretation of Rancid material seems appropriate.

NOFX blitzed through a handful of Rancid tunes in their own sharp, fast, inimitable style. 'I Am the One', 'Olympia WA.', 'Tenderloin' and 'Antennas' all have great musicianship, though Fat Mike wisely resisted copying Matt's more testing bass lines. There is room to move however, and Mike throws a line from Youth Brigade's 'Sink with Kalifornia' into 'Antennas'. The deep 'hey-hey-hey''s thrown in on 'I Am the One', are sublime. NOFX also cover 'Corazon De Oro' from *Life*. Fat Mike mimics Tim's slur: again sublime! However, the best moment from NOFX was their cover of that crucial Rancid song: 'Radio'. They do an entirely different version, opting for a reggae interpretation, slowed right down, with a deep bass line giving it authenticity. It has a smirk, of course. The melody truly comes through, each word easy to hear courtesy of a lovely vocal from guitarist El Hefe.

'Moron Brothers' (Fat Mike)

One of my favourite NOFX numbers, with wit and quirky nuances throughout. However, Rancid's tracks have never really had many quirky nuances – the musicianship would stray into jazzy interludes, for example. Right from the trademark 'Let's go' cry, Tim takes the lead, his gritty sneer obviously different to Fat Mike's higher-pitched, clear, whiny tone. The chorus has a nice NOFX vocal impersonation courtesy of Tim and Lars though: all bright and Californian. Rancid basically charge through the track with a full, distorted, heavy guitar attack. Matt's distorted bass and revised line, ramps things up further. There are no jazzy 'doo-doo''s as on the original. Thus, no light and shade, or quirky nuance. And it's shorter.

The Moron Brothers were in fact a bluegrass duo, who, coincidentally, also produced songs stuffed full of humour and sarcasm. But this song isn't about them, reportedly being about the band's drummer Eric Sandin and his roadie buddy. Sandin was a junkie in the early-1990s, and his behaviour at parties would include pissing in ice trays and generally causing as much chaos as possible. So, Fat Mike christened the pair the Moron Brothers. The original appeared on 1991's *Ribbed*.

'Stickin' In My Eye' (Fat Mike)

Another top song. It seemed to be everywhere a few years back. It was originally from the *White Trash, Two Heebs And A Bean* album. The original vocal arrangement and harmonies on the chorus were superb. Lars takes the lead vocal here, and as Rancid have always had excellent vocal arrangements, the chorus harmonies are handled easily. The buzz-saw guitars are beefed up, but otherwise, it's a faithful rendition of a cool punk rock song.

'Bob' (Fat Mike)

A logical choice of song for Rancid to cover, with a lyric about addicts, complete with 'Oi' chants. It sounds like it could be a Rancid song. Again, the band decided to omit the jazzy interludes in favour of a more-straightforward approach all the way through. Tim's gargled vocal cements the Rancid sonic further. This was originally from the *White Trash, Two Heebs and A Bean* LP.

'Don't Call Me White' (Fat Mike)

This is one of NOFX's most famous songs, obviously. It was a single taken from 1994's classic *Punk in Drublic*. Its subject matter – reverse racism and the rejection of the white stereotype – is typical of Fat Mike's sharp lyrics.

Matt takes the lead vocal – his well-rounded growl some distance from Mike's vocal style, to say the least. It takes some getting used to on such a well-known song as this. However, his performance does work. Matt's unique vocal accentuates the lyric's anger and frustration. He sounds as if he could've been the song's original protagonist.

'The Brews' (Fat Mike)
Another obvious NOFX track for Rancid to tackle, with its street-punk touches and 'Oi' chants. What a great song this is. Again, from the classic *Punk in Drublic* album.

This is the best Rancid cover on the disc. The original's natural kick is given greater emphasis by Brett Reed: his drums sharp in the mix. It's also faster and more aggressive, with Rancid's natural gang-like spirit, emanating. Lars rises to the occasion, as ever, as lead vocalist. Matt manages to slide in some impressive four-string bass technique, his playing sounding like a solo at times. It's not particularly street punk, possibly, but he more than gets away with it.

'Vanilla Sex' (Fat Mike)
This is adolescent humour but has a message within. A teenage boy has his right to privacy, playtime and pornography, right? Anti-censorship, human rights, liberty and freedom-of-speech-and-expression are all on the line. 'Vanilla Sex' tackles the whole lot within its clever metaphor.

Lars' vocal does the theme justice. Indeed, he takes the spirit of the lyric and moves it to a deeper level, sounding very personal. He does a good line in troubadour-style singing, and a righteous theme such as this deserves his committed performance. It's Rancid we're talking about here: commitment is a given. This was originally a song from the Brett Gurewitz-produced *S&M Airlines* album.

133

Stand-alone Singles

These were released independently of Rancid's studio albums – a value-for-money tactic that many used in punk's early days.

'Brad Logan'/'Brad Logan' (Excerpt)/'Brad Logan' (Excerpt)
Personnel:
Tim Armstrong, Lars Frederiksen: guitar, vocals
Matt Freeman: bass, vocals
Brett Reed: drums
Producers: Tim Armstrong, Lars Frederiksen, Rick Rubin
Label: American Records
Release date: 1999
Chart position: Did not chart

'Brad Logan' (Armstrong)
A song about the former Rancid roadie, F-Minus guitarist and frontman, and Leftover Crack member Brad Logan aka Brad Minus. The song was recorded for the cartoon series *South Park* and was included on the 1998 album *Chef Aid*. Rancid appeared as cartoon images in the show's second series.

The single was released as a promo to the *Chef Aid* album.

The song was recorded during the band's most experimental period: the 1998 *Life* sessions. Light and shade, deeply resonant guitar licks, unusual instrumentation (a clavinet played by Eric Stefani) and rimshot verses, all combine with Lars delivering a terrific vocal. The inevitable big chorus, highlights the Anaheim location. Despite the drug references, it has a bright sonic. Wonderful stuff.

'Sick Sick World'/'Young Al Capone'/'Antennas'
Personnel:
Tim Armstrong, Lars Frederiksen: guitar, vocals
Matt Freeman: bass, vocals
Brett Reed: drums
Producer: Brett Gurewitz
Label: Rancid Records
Release date: 9 December 2003
Released as a limited-edition 12" on white and clear vinyl in America only.

A-side
'Young Al Capone' (Armstrong, Frederiksen)
Yes, despite not being on the front cover, 'Young Al Capone' is on the A-side. The same version as the album.

B-side
'Antennas' (Armstrong)
Same as the album.

'Sick Sick World' (Armstrong)
This could've been on *Rancid 5*: its aggressive, spitting hardcore would've fit right in. Matt's bass introduction opens the door for a ferocious assault, led by Tim's snarling, sneering, gargled vocal. It's really short, clocking in at just over a minute, including a bass solo. Rancid's approach is refreshing in guitar music. It obviously helps having a bass player like Matt Freeman whose capable of providing an amazing bass solo. It means a predictable guitar solo doesn't have to be used every time.

Cock Sparrer. 'England Belongs to Me, Rancid'/'East Bay Night'
Personnel.
Tim Armstrong, Lars Frederiksen: guitar, vocals
Matt Freeman: bass, vocals
Braden Steineckert: drums
Label: Pirate Press
Producer: Brett Gurewitz
London's Cock Sparrer – formed in 1972 – were busy celebrating their 40th anniversary as a band. Their 1982 album *Shock Troops* is an essential item in anyone's punk rock collection. 2012 marked Rancid's 20th year, and the two bands decided to come together on vinyl with this 7", which was issued at a series of gigs in December 2012. One show took place in San Francisco, where 1000 copies of the red vinyl version were made available. Another took place in Birmingham, England, where 300 copies were up for grabs on coloured vinyl. Finally, a further 1000 copies were on offer at London shows.

A-side
'England Belongs To Me' (Cock Sparrer)
An updated version of their classic anthem of belonging. Recorded in 2012.

B-side
'East Bay Night' (Rancid)
Rancid went for something from their own catalogue displaying their roots. The version is the same as on the album.

'Sheena Is a Punk Rocker' (Ramones)
Personnel:
Tim Armstrong, Lars Frederiksen: guitar, vocals
Matt Freeman: bass
Brett Reed: drums

Label: Pirate Press
Producer: Rancid

A blistering cover of the Ramones classic. It has street-punk elements and hardcore touches. It was included as a free single-sided flexi-disc giveaway by Pirate Press Records, as part of the 2012 *Essentials* package. The recording was also included on the 2003 Columbia compilation *We're A Happy Family*, which included such acts as Red Hot Chili Peppers, Kiss, The Pretenders and Garbage.

'Turn In Your Badge'/'Something to Believe In A World Gone Mad '

Personnel:
Tim Armstrong, Lars Frederiksen: guitar, vocals
Matt Freeman: bass, vocals
Branden Steineckert: drums
Label: Hellcat
Producer: Brett Gurewitz
Release date: 27 October 2014
Chart position: Did not chart

A 7" vinyl release in various colours. Both tracks were included on the *Honor* expanded edition in 2017.

A-side
'Turn In Your Badge' (Rancid)

This could've easily made it onto *Honor,* and certainly stands shoulder-to-shoulder with most of the album's tracks. It's heavy, quick and distorted, with Tim and Lars trading vocals nicely. Matt's bass is resonant, deep and fuzzy, and the guitar solo in the middle, splits its one minute and 15 seconds in two, allowing the song to speed to its finale.

B-side
'Something To Believe in A World Gone Mad' (Rancid)

A rumbling affair. Matt's deep bass works with Branden's tom-toms to decent effect. The call-and-response chorus is easy to follow. But in my opinion, it's not the band's best number, never really reaching the high I associate with Rancid. Maybe the aim was to produce a slightly odd or incomplete number; a kind of work in progress. Maybe they should've let it become part of a bootleg issue on Deadcat Records.

'We Arrived on Time'/'Go on Rise Up'

Personnel:
Tim Timebomb, Lars Frederiksen: guitar, vocals
Matt Freeman: bass, vocals

Branden Steineckert: drums
Label: Hellcat
Producer: Brett Gurewitz
This single was a bonus item issued as part of the expanded edition of *Trouble Maker* in 2017.

A-side
'We Arrived on Time' (Timebomb, Freeman, Frederiksen, Steineckert)

A shuddering song, again well-crafted. A sweet pause prior to the richly voiced chorus, works well, nudging the door open for the rich, deep, harmonious voices singing the title. Its two minutes and 21 seconds are nicely signed off with a guitar solo.

B-side
'Go On Rise Up' (Timebomb)

This is a suggestive number, loaded with bright moments, a pop-tastic backbeat and ringing guitar chords. The lyric is quite sentimental; almost a love song, about rising above (rather than resisting) the world's ills, and making the most of things.

> The world is special
> I just wanna hold you
> The frequency is there
> I just wanna show you

'Oh Oh I Love Her So'/'I'm Against It'

Personnel:
Tim Armstrong, Lars Frederiksen: guitar, vocals
Matt Freeman: bass
Brett Reed: drums
Label: Deadcat
UK Release Date: 14 December 2017
This single was released in limited numbers in Europe, only on Deadcat Records. It's a good one to track down if you can.

A-side
'Oh Oh I Love Her So' (Ramones)

An acoustic version – recorded for radio purposes – of the Ramones classic. Rancid often played it live: full-on, with Lars taking the lead vocal. Here, he still takes the lead and 'ooh''s are reproduced by Tim. Despite the relaxed feel, it has a nice sharp tempo and works very well.

B-side
'I'm Against It' (Ramones)
A full-on rendition of the track from *Road to Ruin*: by Ramones, in case you didn't know. This is fully faithful to the original, with its pulsating wall of sound and Tim taking the lead vocal.

Murphys Law – 'Just One Beer'/ Rancid – 'We're Gonna Figure It Out'
Personnel:
Tim Armstrong, Lars Frederiksen: guitar, vocals
Matt Freeman: bass, vocals
Branden Steineckert: drums
Label: Pitchfork
Producer: Rancid
US Release date: 24 July 2018

This limited edition 7" was released in the US on clear and half-blue/half-black vinyl, and clear vinyl with a red splodge on it. Murphys Law hadn't released an album since 2005. This second incarnation of that band was still fronted by Jimmy Gestapo. 'Just One Beer' carried on the theme in the band's song titles: beer was invariably mentioned! 'Beer Song', 'Attack Of The Killer Beers', 'Beer'.

'We're Gonna Figure It Out' (Armstrong, Frederiksen, Freeman)
A latter-day Rancid treat, with shining, anthemic, melodic guitar dominating the intro and mid-section. There is great vocal interchange from Tim and Lars in the verses: question-and-answer style. The chorus contains massive 'woah''s, and with bass breaks from Matt, it's quintessential Rancid. It's also the band's most recent official release.

Selected Rarities

These recordings are out there, but not necessarily easy to track down.

'The Harder They Come' (Cliff)

Rancid performed their version of Jimmy Cliff's 1971 classic on the road in the 1990s, including at the Tibetan Freedom Concert in 1997. The concert was among a series of events designed to raise awareness and support for Tibetan independence, and Rancid were part of the New York show in June alongside several star names including Radiohead, Lee 'Scratch' Perry and Patti Smith. Rancid were touring *Life* at this time, so the song slotted right in. Capitol Records released a live album of the New York gig – the *Tibetan Freedom Concert* – in November the same year, and Rancid's 'The Harder They Come' was included on the second disc of the three-disc set, sandwiched between the Beastie Boys and Bjork.

Rancid do a thumping version, more up-tempo than Cliff's original, with a brass section joining them on stage. Lars' vocal is thrilling, and frankly he almost steals the show. The recording shows Rancid truly rising to the occasion alongside such illustrious company. The album is still available if you search hard for it, though it's a patchy affair. Rancid, however, are up there with the best.

'Dr Israel vs Rancid Coppers' (Brooklyn version)/'Pressure'/'Armagideon Time' (1999)

This is a hip hop version of *Life*'s final track, released as 'Brooklyn version' on Amethyst Records. Lars' vocal cuts through, and Tim's rap is pushed right up. DJ Israel, toasts – all over a controlled hip hop soundscape. It's heavily vocal, with 'woah''s ubiquitous but effective. There is very little guitar.

It appeared on DJ Israel's superb album *Inna City Pressure*. The album also contained a cover of The Clash's 'Armageddon Time' (without Rancid!).

'Misty Days' - Buju Banton feat. Rancid (Banton, Rancid)

Cracking stuff – Rancid repaying the favour of Buju appearing on *Life*'s title track. The chiming guitars and thunderous drums, fuse with Buju's verse to produce a superb rock/reggae crossover. Buju's gravelly voice does lend itself to this kind of link-up, and the band's backing vocals are sublime.

The track appeared on *Dubbing With The Banton* (1999) and on *Give 'Em The Boot* 2.

'X-Mas Eve (She Got Up And Left Me)' (Armstrong, Frederiksen, Freeman)

This Yuletide ditty was recorded for one of the Christmas charity albums put out by Radio KROQ DJs Kevin and Bean. *Fo' Shizzle St Nizzle* was issued in 2002 on KROQ's own label, featuring comedy skits and recordings by artists such as Good Charlotte and The Flaming Lips. Coldplay contributed 'Have Yourself A Merry Little Christmas'.

Tim's lyric tells a tragic tale of a typical Christmas Eve breakup: 'You said you protect me/And you left me on Christmas Eve/I feel so empty'. The chorus words are sung in unison, Lars taking the verse vocal. The whole thing has a glorious throwaway feel and must've been great fun to knock together. It has resonant lead-guitar licks, with an NYC punk feel. Rancid gave it away as a free download to fans in 2015. Happy holidays, ya hooligans!

'If The Kids Are United' (Pursey, Parsons)
The lead track from the second *Give 'Em The Boot 2* compilation, released in 1999 on Hellcat. It is, of course, Rancid's cover of the 1979 Sham 69 classic. Rancid's version is a little too bass-focussed for me. Matt's runs are as impressive as ever, but they come close to dominating proceedings. The slashing riff is still there, Lars sings with passion in the verses, but the chorus has bass notes almost working against the vocal. To me, this chorus should be a terrace chant – arms in the air, fists clenched, allowing the message of unity to be delivered without complication or compromise.

'Fuck You' (Rancid)
An absolute barroom banger. The opening rock-'n'-roll boogie-guitar-rhythm riff is like Status Quo on speed. It's richly distorted and simple. A rock-'n'-roll bass pattern, underpins proceedings. The retro rock-'n'-roll is fused with Lars' melodic guitar-playing and a fuck-you attitude. Pure Oi!. Pure street punk. A real live favourite.

> We say what we want
> We do what we want
> We live like we want
> So, everyone singin' with us – fuck you!

The lyric justifies and celebrates coming out of a shitty neighbourhood and doing what you want with your life. And in Rancid's case, this was to play live, from squats to arenas.

The track originally appeared on the 2012 compilation *Oi! This Is Street Punk Volume 2*: released on Pirate Press on 12 December 2012. Rancid issued 'Fuck You' as a download six days later. It was also included on the cracking 2018 compilation *One Family One Flag*: a triple album – again released by Pirate Press – including Argy Bargy, Cock Sparrer, The Interrupters and Street Dogs.

Compilation Albums
B-Sides and C-Sides (LP) (2007)

This was released on Rancid Records on CD only in 2008. If you buy one Rancid compilation – assuming you have all the studio albums – then make it this one. It plugged a gap between *Indestructible* (2003 and *Dominoes* (2009). This compilation was released with the minimum of fuss and was well-received.

It neatly packages together B-sides, unreleased cuts and rarities – not an original tactic by any means: think The Clash's *Super Black Market Clash* collection. But mopping up these recordings provided a service to the Rancid fan. This compilation was improved further when an expanded version came out including the entire debut EP. Finally, a vinyl issue came out in 2013, with 'Blacklisted', 'X-Mas Eve (She Got Up And Left Me)' and 'Fuck You' on it. Check the rarities section of the book for details of these tracks. In my opinion it would've made a lot of sense to also include the original version of 'Radio' and 'Someone's Gunna Die Tonight' from the *Radio Radio Radio* EP. 'Just A Feeling' from the same EP *was* included, for example. There are other omissions: notably the cover of 'If The Kids Are United'.

Nevertheless, it is a cracking compilation. Please note that not all songwriting credits are available.

'Ben Zanotto' (Armstrong, Frederiksen)
Same version as on the B-side of 'Let Me Go' (2000).

'Stop' (Armstrong)
Same version as on B-Side of 'Bloodclot' (1998).

'Devil's Dance' (Unknown)
Completely unreleased, recorded during the 1998 *Life* sessions. Given the album's diversity, there could've been room for a second 1950s pastiche like this. If you like 'Lady Liberty', 'Young Al Capone' and the psychobilly side of Rancid, then you'll love this. There's sharp, nifty, clear-as-a-bell guitar twang from Lars, upright bass slap from Matt, and rimshot-based rhythm from Brett Reed.

The guitar-playing is the standout. Not just the bends and hammer-ons, but the damping, single-string runs and weaving-in-and-out. Lars' voice is strong and masculine, and so suits rockabilly. Female voices perform the backing vocals: uncommon on the band's work.

The lyric's theme is danger and temptation, often masked by outward appearance, like a Devil's dance. There is positivity – the hope of the female protagonist to get clean of drugs and alcohol. But with temptation around every cover, it ain't easy.

She gonna go
She gonna seek and destroy

She gonna split with the whole damn scene
Make a run, cause some rebellion
Hustle some cash with the danger eyes

Great tune, which sounds like a Tim and Lars collaboration, possibly with
Matt chipping in too given his work with Devils Brigade. I can't be sure of this,
however.

'Dead And Gone' (Armstrong, Frederiksen)
Same version as on B-Side of 'Let Me Go' (2000).

'Stranded' (Armstrong, Frederiksen)
Same version as on B-Side of 'Fall Back Down' (2003).

'Killing Zone' (Armstrong, Frederiksen)
Same version as on B-Side of 'Fall Back Down'.

'100 Years' (Unknown)
Completely unreleased, and again from the *Life* sessions. It's a rare
instrumental, with a surf-style single-string guitar riff leading the way. The
guitar melody sounds almost as if played straight into the mixing desk: again,
typical of the band's experimentation in 1998.
    It's an exhilarating white-knuckle ride, soaring with chord changes. Possibly a
group collaboration, writing-wise.

'Things To Come' (Armstrong)
Same version as on the B-Side of 'Hooligans' (1998).

'Blast 'Em' (Armstrong, Frederiksen, Freeman)
Same version as on the B-side of 'Timebomb' in 1995. It was also included on
the 1996 Epitaph compilation *Bored Generation*.

'Endrina' (Armstrong)
Same recording as on B-Side of 'Bloodclot'.

'White Knuckle Ride' (Armstrong)
Two words: Matt Freeman. Is this the man's most mind-bending bass line? His
playing is, frankly, incredible. The tempo is world-record level; the finger work,
precise; the feel, on the money. The introductory runs alone are breathtaking:
the listener cannot focus on much else.
    That said, Tim's vocal is throaty and gutsy. His lyric is open to interpretation,
and no interview mentions the song and its inspiration. Guns are referenced,
as are drugs, so the white-knuckle ride that is life – with its temptation, risk and

downfall – is one explanation. At 87 seconds in length, there isn't time for too much lyric content, especially with Mr. Freeman's bass-playing taking centre stage.

This was originally included on the 1999 Disaster Records compilation *Old Skars and Upstarts*.

'Sick Sick World' (Armstrong)

Same version as on the 2000 12" single. Also appeared on the 2001 *Warped Tour* compilation.

'Tattoo' (Armstrong)

Originally included on the soundtrack to Taylor Steele's 1998 surf film *The Show*; released on Theologian Records. This was also the opening cut on *Give 'Em The Boot 5*. It's a deep song with a Lars vocal that's a *tour de force*.

It's a personal lyric; very introspective, yet easy to dismiss as superficial, as the subject matter is a tattoo. The permanence and affirmation made by getting ink done, is obvious: it's a commitment of fidelity, style, character; it's for life and is not just decoration. It's real. The tattoo is a metaphor for loyalty, commitment and friendship. The song is most likely about Tim's relationship with Brody Dalle. Tim had a tattoo of her name.

As on a track like 'The War's End' from *Wolves*, Lars does a great line in troubadour singing. He delivers the words with passion; with sincerity.

'That's Entertainment' (Armstrong, Frederiksen, Freeman)

Same version as on B-Side of 'Ruby Soho' (1995).

'Clockwork Orange' (Unknown)

This is arguably the album highlight, with a real bite to match its streetwise sonic. It's dark and gritty with a killer chorus, and inexplicably unreleased until now.

Discordant guitar kicks it off, signalling the second guitar to begin chord-slashing. Tim and Lars' vocals combine superbly, especially on the chorus and harmonies. Tim does the low register, Lars the high. The sonic is unsettling. Sirens wail, guitars feed back, and eerie space is permitted as chords are left to ring.

This is what Stanley Kubrick's movie is all about, of course. Rancid's 'Clockwork Orange' is written from the perspective of someone who's about to go on an anarchistic crime binge with the film's main character Alex. It even refers to the car Alex and his cronies steal early in the film: a Durango '95: 'Apocalypse now, static on the run/It's just me and Alex on a Durango '95'. Like on 'Sidekick' from *Let's Go*, Tim uses a film to let his imagination roll. It's streetwise, snarling, and the compilation's best track. A whole host of acts – from David Bowie to Blur, and even Guns N' Roses – have taken inspiration from *A Clockwork Orange*: 'Clockwork Orange fighting dogs in the queue/It's just me and Alex watching shit, breaking too'.

The song has Tim Armstrong's quality as a lyricist all over it, taking a cultural theme and exploring it. The rest of the band could well have contributed to the music, of course. But the actual writing credit isn't revealed.

'The Brothels' (Armstrong, Frederiksen)

This was included on the very first Hellcat *Give 'Em The Boot* compilation, in 1997. It's a kick-ass punk rock song. A Chuck Berry-esque top-B-and-E-string guitar riff, along with more slashing chords, create a distorted guitar attack which raise the hairs on the back of the neck. Maybe it's down to the obvious Steve Jones-esque wall-of-sound-style riff.

It's a street lyric, using Willie as a main character who knew the prostitutes working in the brothels, had access to speed and other narcotics, and could get his hands on plenty more. A picture of urban life, underage drinking and the police lying in wait. Willie then begged for forgiveness. The latter point could apply to too much of the seedy side of life, I guess.

> And when I first did him, I knew he was tough
> And not to my surprise, he liked it rough
> Red leather pants, a tattooed neck
> And prayin' hard to Jesus, sayin' give him a rest

It's sequenced beautifully on the record, with sirens linking the fiction of 'Clockwork Orange' to the truth of 'The Brothels'.

'Just A Feeling' (Armstrong, Freeman)

Same as the version on *Radio Radio Radio* EP (1993).

'Brixton' (Armstrong, Frederiksen, Freeman)

A great song, included on the *Kill Rock Stars* compilation. The melodic chorus is one of the band's best. It also provides a history lesson. Being from England, I clearly remember the 1990s poll-tax riots which broke out nationwide: notably in Brixton, London. Margaret Thatcher's Conservative government planned to impose a new kind of tax, replacing the personal rating system. It was called the poll tax and was designed to make the poor pay the same as the rich, no matter how big or small the dwelling. Thus, a rich person in their mansion paid the same as a poor one in their humble home. How can that be fair? So, fair play to Rancid: an American band getting their heads around a British problem.

The Clash's influence is never far away; Joe Strummer and Paul Simonon were there from the first brick at the Brixton race riots of 1976. Of course, despite the song title, it isn't exclusively about rioting in the UK. Oakland has had its fair share, such as the 1960s ones mentioned in 'Telegraph Avenue'.

'Brixton' is melodic and optimistic, despite this. Riots are positive things when there's a good purpose. It's your democratic right as a human being, and it gives you hope. And it opens the door for other less admirable opportunism, or equalisation, maybe.

Don't pay the poll tax, the headlines read
Thirty cops beaten, another one dead
The fight lasted on 'til the break of the night
A thousand angry looters who knew they were right

'Empros Lap Dog' (Unknown)
Another unreleased cut from the *Life* sessions. The fact that songs from these sessions are included here for the first time, shows how prolific and daring the band were in 1998. Furthermore, it's another example of Rancid shining a light on worldwide political situations: in this case the troubles in East Timor. In the late-1990s, the population sought and voted for independence from Indonesia.

It's a lightning-quick, manic ska-punk workout, with brass, frenetic guitar and bass, and terrific backing vocals. A well-crafted piece of work. Matt's bass drops in a busy groove, and Tim delivers a laconic, slurry lead vocal that sits right on top of the high-speed backing, balanced perfectly with the sound.

'I Wanna Riot' (Armstrong, Frederiksen, Freeman)
Same as the B-Side of 'Roots Radicals' (1995). Also included on the first *Punk-O-Rama* compilation in 1994.

'Kill The Lights' (Unknown)
A second cut from Disaster Records' 1999 *Old Skars and Upstarts* compilation. It's 86 seconds long and is as pissed off and angry as Rancid ever sounded.

Bonus Tracks included on the 2008 expanded edition
'I'm Not The Only One', 'Battering Ram', 'The Sentence', 'Media Controller', 'Idle Hands'.
The 2013 double-vinyl release also included the following three tracks.

'Blacklisted' (Armstrong)
From the 1999 *Short Music For Short People* compilation released on Fat Wreck Chords. The album had 101 pieces of music, each lasting less than a minute. The likes of The Damned, The Offspring, Less than Jake and loads more were involved. 'Blacklisted' is 27 seconds long, brutal, and in line with the *Rancid 5* era. The theme is those in authority deciding people are unimportant, and effectively blacklisting them.

The other two tracks are both covered in the 'Rarities' section and are 'X-Mas Eve (She Got Up And Left Me)' and 'Fuck You'.

Essentials (2012)

Rancid don't do *normal* compilations. In 2012, *Essentials* was issued by Californian Punk Label Pirate Press Records. The package included each album up to and including 2009's *Dominoes* – not in itself unusual, as many bands who've been around for a while have released boxed sets. But what we're looking at here is one with a difference. The music from the seven studio albums, EPs and the *B-Sides And C-Sides* collection was spread out over 46 7" singles. So that's 92 sides of vinyl in total. The acoustic tracks from the *Dominoes* expanded edition were also included. This was all presented in a robust, cool, leather DJ-style flight box, resplendent with Rancid logo and artwork. Furthermore, all cuts were remastered, and frankly, sounded fantastic. 2012 heralded the band's 20th anniversary, see.

Each album had between four and six 7" discs accommodating the tracks, except for *Dominoes*, which had eight discs due to the acoustic cuts. Each album had new, updated artwork, and for Rancid collectors, these soon became prized items. The box-sets were limited to a total of 2000, on red, and red-and-white vinyl. Yes, it was expensive: nearly 300 quid. But you could get hold of each album's singles separately if you wished, and they still crop up on the vinyl market.

The only new (ish) track was the cover of 'Sheena Is A Punk Rocker'. It was put on a flexi disc accompanying the box set. Remember though, it was included on Columbia's 2003 *We're A Happy Family* Ramones covers compilation, so *unreleased* it ain't.

Note that none of the *Essentials* content is treated in this book as a properly issued *single*.

All The Moon Stompers (2015)

A popular compilation issued in 2014. The title is obviously a line from 'Roots Radicals', and one could be forgiven for thinking the compilation was a *best-of* type thing, but no.

This 2015 collection was originally the brainchild of Daryl Smith: guitarist with Cock Sparrer and Argy Bargy. Daryl curated the album. His sleeve notes are a great read, recounting how for years he burnt tracks off CDs to make ska compilations of Rancid's finest skanking sounds. He titled these *Radio Ska, Hooligans, Roots, Roots And Offbeats* and *Lars Is A Cunt*. Daryl had a close relationship (obviously) with Lars, see. The pair worked together with Argy Bargy in 2006, and Daryl approached Lars with the idea of putting a compilation out. Nothing came of it. But in 2013, after the Cock Sparrer and Rancid anniversary shows, Lars called Daryl up. It was on.

Rather than put *All The Moon Stompers* out through Epitaph, the band chose the German punk label and home to The Old Firm Casuals: Randale Records. Initially, it was available on vinyl only, but eventually came out on CD via Chase The Ace. Daryl eventually got his wish: an official ska compilation from Rancid. No need to keep burning CDs for his car journeys.

The collection itself – though a cracking listen – was comprised solely of material recorded and included on the band's first seven albums, a rarity or two, and a few B-Sides. All tracks had been released before, and obscure ones had already been mopped up on *B-Sides And C-Sides*. Thus, there's nothing new on *All The Moon Stompers*.

The cover art is great – depicting a club scene in cartoon form, featuring stereotypical ska fans: suede heads, skinhead girls, a spiky punk clutching a 'Time Bomb' 45, and a stitched-up skin resplendent in a Cock Sparrer t-shirt. A coincidence, of course. The layout was by Daryl; the drawings by Alteau.

Live Albums

Rancid have never issued a full official live album – adopting the Joe Strummer policy of not releasing a live record while the band were consistently playing live. However, there are live recordings available. Between 2006 and 2008, a whole bunch of shows (37, in fact) were issued as downloads to fans on www. jrae.com, with the following disclaimer:

> Recorded directly from the soundboard in multi-channel format, and mixed in a studio environment. Never before has Rancid's energy and spontaneity been captured from the stage and offered to you, the fan.

Some boast, eh? A fan could get a recording of the show they'd attended if they were lucky. In my case: Rock City, Nottingham, in November 2007.

Most of these recordings are no longer commercially available. Some live recordings are, however, and here are some significant ones, in my view. I will list them chronologically by date of performance rather than date of release.

Demolition Sessions (LP) (1994)

Ten live numbers from a gig on 23 June 1993 at Gilman Street are included on this bootleg. Lars had just joined Rancid, and this is one of his earliest shows. It's an intense performance. The tracks are, 'Rejected', 'I'm Not The Only One', 'Adina', 'Media Controller', 'Detroit', 'Dope Sick Girl', 'Trenches', 'The Sentence', 'Whirlwind', 'Animosity'.

See Ya In The Pit (LP) (2013)

Released on the Italian label Buy Or Die Records. This catches the raw intensity, chaos and ferocity of the band live in 1995: recorded at The Garage, London. Although the recording quality isn't refined, it's still enjoyable, warts and all. For example, when Lars starts up 'The War's End', the crowd serenade him with a chorus of 'You fat bastard': a term of endearment reserved for many punk heroes. It seemed to render the band speechless. Wonderful. The banter between band and crowd is great throughout. Tim is humble when he expresses gratitude for anyone coming to both London shows. He also says he might lose his front tooth with all the moshing prior to 'Radio'. The song then turns into a riot.

Rancid sound tight, and their ability to reproduce the vocal harmonies live on stage, is commendable. They blast through material from the EPs and the first three albums. The version of 'Time Bomb' early in the set is a longer arrangement with repeated verses and guitar solo. There's a rampage through 'Rejected' later on, and the album closes with support band Swinging Utters joining the band on stage as they do Blitz's 'Someone's Gonna Die Tonight'. It's a great finale.

'See Ya In The Pit' is the band's message to fans on their album sleeve notes, of course. This bootleg is very much from the pit: a place where band and fans unite.

Live In the Drive (BB Kings NYC, 2006)
One of the live downloads issued in the early 2000s, and in this case, released on vinyl by Deadcat Records. A limited number were on coloured vinyl, but these seem to be readily available at record fairs and online retailers.

The show was recorded at BB Kings in New York City in August 2006. The 37 songs are spread over four sides of vinyl: it was a double-album bootleg, see. Three Op Ivy numbers – 'Knowledge', 'Big City' and 'Sound System' – are present, as is 'Skunx' from Lars Frederiksen and the Bastards' debut record. The Rancid songs are taken from all releases up to and including *Indestructible*.

You're Not Invited (LP) (2006)
Not a live show in front of an audience, but one for radio, hence its inclusion here as a live bootleg. It was initially a download, but like the *Live In The Drive* bootleg, ended up being packaged onto a Deadcat physical release in December 2006.

Brett Reed plays guitar and sings. This is a recording of an acoustic performance made for Fungus 53 XM Radio, Washington, on 18 August 2006. It was one of Brett's final contributions prior to his departure. It's available on CD only.

Following an introduction from DJ Lou Brutus, the setlist is as follows: 'Memphis', 'Fall Back Down', 'Olympia WA.', 'Listed MIA', 'Roots Radicals', 'Sound System', 'Wrongful Suspicion', 'The 11th Hour'. The disc closes with an outro by Brutus. 'Sound System' has two takes.

Dead End Sessions (LP) (2015)
Another acoustic radio performance, this time for Seattle's WA, recorded on 6 July 2009. Again, originally a download.

Track listing: 'East Bay Nights', 'Adina', 'Maxwell Murder', 'The 11th Hour', 'L.A. River', 'Harry Bridges', 'St. Mary', 'Civilian Ways', 'New Orleans', 'Who Would've Thought', 'Tenderloin', 'The Highway', 'Ruby Soho'.

Selected Studio Bootlegs

Once again, I will focus on bootlegs I feel are worth getting hold of. There's quite a lot of duplication out there.

Demos From the Pit (LP) (1995)

A selection of early demos, taken 1992-1994: aka the *Lookout!* years when the band were a three-piece. The same bootleg recordings were also released under the moniker *Give 'Em the Boot*. Ten tracks were recorded for the band's debut EP, but only five were selected to go on it, so it's interesting to see what got rejected. The band are well-rehearsed, and the demos that did make the cut are not especially different arrangement-wise to the final recordings. I love the clear, sharp sirens in 'Animosity': roughly mixed. 'Trenches' sounds identical to the album. There are two demos of 'Unwritten Rules'.

However, more interesting are those tracks not selected for either the EP or LP. I haven't been able to ascertain accurate writing credits, but it's reasonable to assume most are in line with the band's debut album – words by Tim Armstrong, music by Rancid.

'To Hell'

A track from the *Rancid* sessions. An incendiary punk run-out, full of vitriol and vocal interchange between Matt and Tim.

'Opposition'

Another track from the *Rancid* sessions. It's slower, with lighter, spacey verses, and a steady build leading to a full-on snarling chorus. Matt's bass-playing is again to the fore, as normal on the band's early material. This was played live at the band's 1992 gigs.

'Inhalation'

Brutal, quick, riffy, and full of bass technique. I'm surprised it didn't make any of the band's early releases, though the finale needs tidying up.

'Borderline'

This does sound as if it could even get onto *Let's Go*. It's more accessible, cleaner, with an easily comprehended vocal. It's a strong hint of the direction the band would head in with Lars on board.

'Institution'

This opens with guitar bombs and a solo break. It's reminiscent of 'Black And Blue', and was possibly a work-in-progress of the *Let's Go* number.

'Moonlight'
A rocker, again showing a band with more in their locker than angry street punk.

'Situation'
An early working of 'Union Blood', the unlisted track from *Rancid*. The Clash's influence is even more prevalent, with English-style vocals in the chorus, plus woops and cheers in the background.

'Bad Policeman'
The lead vocal is by Matt, and has the kind of chorus raw punk audiences love, delivered with a kind of 1950s doo-wop vocal: only, on speed.

'Take You'
This has a hint of both 'Adina' and 'Radio' in its verse. The chorus is a little weak, which is possibly why it was dismantled, with the best bits ending up in other songs.

'The Line'
Trashy gutter punk, with a UK influence. There's a great gutsy vocal from Tim, with Matt leading the chorus.

'Burn The City Down'
A spoken-verse vocal from Tim, with Matt taking the chorus. It's a good song, catchy, and it worked live, I guess, though I've never seen them perform it.

Demolition Sessions (LP) (1994)
A good value bootleg, with demos of tracks that appeared on *Let's Go* and *Wolves*. The sessions took place in 1993 and 1994. Also included are the ten tracks recorded live at Gilman Street in June 1993. So, as a document, it has significance, as it follows on from *Demos From The Pit*. Released on Deadcat Records.

The first half-dozen tracks are outtakes from the *Radio Radio Radio* sessions of 1993, and include all tracks from the EP, plus 'The Ballad Of Jimmy And Johnny' and 'Tenderloin'. The remaining demos are from 1994 and are titled the *Roots Radicals Demos*. There are work-in-progress versions of 'Roots Radicals', 'Disorder And Disarray', 'The Way I Feel' and 'Blast 'Em'. But again, the unreleased cuts are more interesting though once again, no full writing credits are available for these songs.

'Ghost Dance'
Matt's busy bass and vocal growl, dominate this rocker. Wall-of-sound guitars fill out the sound. It's probably not the band's greatest moment, but it's not at all bad either.

'Sabrina'
Solid mid-tempo rocking stuff, quite complete, with loud terrace-chant vocals. Rock-'n'-roll guitar solos abound, and Tim's voice sounds fabulous. This could've easily made it onto a later album.

'Do You Wanna Dance With Me' (Armstrong, Frederiksen)
Aka 'Little Rude Girl'. A complete recording, with lead vocal from Lars. It's a simple song about a girl in a red dress, who the protagonist would like to get close to, to dance with and maybe, date. But he realises that the girl probably doesn't want to reciprocate. It's up-tempo and fun. The song deservedly saw the light of day (as 'Little Rude Girl') courtesy of Lars Frederiksen And The Bastards. A hidden gem, I'd say.

'End Of The World Tonight'
Tim takes the lead vocal on a scorching track, inexplicably left off any official release. It has great guitar, vocal and chorus, with a lyric about the end of the world, but not really, if you get my drift. The clean lead guitar seems at odds with the rest of the muscular guitar distortion.

'My Life (Sick Of It All)'
63 seconds of intensity. A version of the 'Sick Of It All' number from the band's *Blood, Sweat And No Tears* album. Matt sings, and is, frankly, awesome.

'Leave It To Tomorrow' (The Frumpies)
This has the regular ingredients: big chorus, raucous guitar, total commitment. It's not necessarily a standout, though it's decent. The Frumpies featured members of Bikini Kill.

BBC Sessions (7", 1996)
A single containing four tracks recorded in 1995 for BBC Radio 1 at the Maida Vale studios. There's an absolutely barnstorming version of 'Roots Radicals', rocking like nothing on earth. It's brilliant, with alternative words through the megaphone prior to the mid-section. 'She's Automatic' continues in a similar manner: the band clearly in prime form. 'Time Bomb' has the extended arrangement version the band were using live in 1995. There are repeated verses and an additional rip-roaring guitar solo. Lars plays the Hammond break on guitar. It rolls and skanks in all its finery. 'Junkie Man' is better than on the album, in my opinion. It has more punk energy and is less ethereal.

Life Won't Wait Demo Sessions (LP) (2014)
Another release on Deadcat. It's actually a split between Rancid and The Silencers. The latter were another side project, comprised of Tim, Lars, Vic

Ruggiero, Josh Freese and Cris Quialiana. They crossed mod style ('The Last Mod') with Jamaican-infused sunshine ('Candy', 'Express Yourself').

Rancid demos include 'Brad Logan': not actually on *Life,* but issued as a single, and it appeared on the *Chef Aid* record. The demo has female backing vocals emphasising the chorus. It's very clearly a work in progress, but that's what demos are. Another track left off the original album – 'Things To Come' – is getting towards completion, however, and shows a song further down the production line. The brass, keys and rhythms are in place, with the vocals in need of completion

It's fascinating to hear how a track is built, and these demos show this. They aren't just full songs being rehearsed, but construction projects. *Life* is a more textured album, and the band were becoming expert craftsmen at this point. It also shows the open approach the band had in 1998. 'Backslide' is a cracking example: stark and piano-led, rather than the brassed-out extravaganza that ended up on *Life.* Likewise, 'The Wolf' has Jerry Lee Lewis-style piano drive, and is even rawer 'Who Would've Thought' shows how the band focussed on backing vocals from an early stage. It's an old-school ska workout, highlighting a wonderful song. All demos here have an *around-the-piano* feel, and are different to the band's punk bootlegs.

Let's Go ... Wolves – Demo Sessions (LP) (2015)

Another release on Deadcat. All listed tracks were already released on *Demolition Sessions.* Three more work-in-progress items – 'Time Bomb', 'She's Automatic' and 'Junkie Man' – also feature, but are not listed.

Epilogue

Rancid are very-much still together, and following the Covid-19 pandemic, managed an extensive 2021 co-headline tour with Dropkick Murphys. Sadly, a scheduled 2022 visit to the UK to headline the Slam Dunk festival was shelved, but hopefully, the band will make a return to these shores in the future. However, Lars imparted some good news to *Kerrang* in a November 2021 interview: 'Rancid's putting the finishing touches to a new record as we speak. When that's gonna come out, I'm not so sure'.

Lars himself put out the excellent solo *To Victory* EP in 2021, taking on the Billy Bragg-style troubadour role: something I've always felt he had in his locker. In the same *Kerrang* interview, he confessed, 'It was on my bucket list as a pipe dream'. Tim continues to produce material – notably 2020's *Life's For Livin'* EP, which included the title track, 'It's Quite Alright' and 'The Times They Are A-Changin''. His world seems full of art, media and music, so keep an eye on *timtimebomb.com* for updates.

Matt has recently been involved with Californian punk band The Vulturas, playing on the track 'Bastard Sons'. There's been nothing new from Devil's Brigade since *Trouble Maker* came out, incidentally (and sadly). Branden doesn't seem to do too much in the way of side projects, but his social media sites are a great follow for any fan.

So, hopefully, and in the best possible way, this book will soon become slightly outdated when the band release their next album. Rancid, to me, are one of the most important punk bands of all time. Their devotion to the cause, the quality of their output and the thrill of their live show are without question. Long may that continue. All of us moon stompers, punk rockers and hooligans need you, guys.

The Damned - *on track*
every album, every song

Morgan Brown
Paperback
128 pages
40 colour photographs
978-1-78951-136-8
£14.99
$21.95

Every album and every song by this legendary and long-serving British punk band.

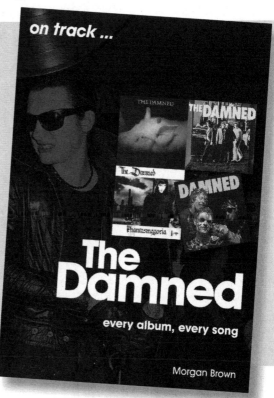

The Damned are a great British rock n' roll institution. They have helped to plot the course of guitar music over the last 45 years, putting UK punk on record for the first time in 1976, and going on to lay the groundwork for the hardcore, Goth, post-punk, indie-pop and horror-punk movements that have thrived in their wake. Ever underestimated by critics, their string of classic albums has nevertheless been hugely influential, from the trailblazing punk of *Damned Damned Damned* to the epic, eclectic sprawl of *The Black Album*, through the glossy dark-pop of *Phantasmagoria*, to the genre-spanning triumph of the recent *Evil Spirits* and beyond.

In this book, Morgan Brown takes a fascinating, deep dive into each of the band's groundbreaking records, unearthing the stories and inspirations behind them. He picks apart their musical building blocks and examines both the creative process and the creators themselves; early visionary leader Brian James, iconic frontman Dave Vanian, madcap genius Captain Sensible, volatile percussive dervish Rat Scabies and many more. Curious new listeners and long-time enthusiasts alike will find this book the perfect companion on a voyage of discovery into the strange, chaotic, wonderful world of The Damned.

The Clash - *on track*
every album, every song

Nick Assirati
Paperback
144 pages
35 colour photographs
978-1-78951-081-1
£14.99
$21.95

Every album and every song by this legendary English punk band.

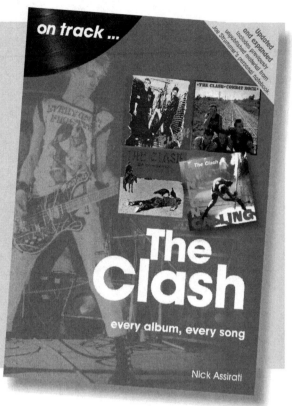

The Clash were an extraordinary band. Bursting out of the punk explosion in 1977, they recorded their self-titled first album over three weekends. It is now regarded as the quintessential punk record. Over the next five years they recorded another fourteen sides of long-playing vinyl including the platinum double-LP *London Calling*, which was voted the best album of the 1980s and the eighth best album of all time by *Rolling Stone* magazine. Through the triple-LP *Sandinista!* to their double-platinum *Combat Rock* plus a whole bunch of stand-alone singles and EPs, The Clash mixed both street and global politics with music spanning several genres including Rock, Reggae, Jazz, Rap, Calypso and Rockabilly.

This book provides a concise narrative of the rise and fall of The Clash, putting each song of their prolific musical output into context, including a selection of bootlegs and rarities. There is also advice about how to buy The Clash's music without falling into the record company trap of repeatedly buying the same material through different compilations, making this the most essential guide to the music of this iconic band yet written.

On Track series

Alan Parsons Project – Steve Swift 978-1-78952-154-2
Tori Amos – Lisa Torem 978-1-78952-142-9
Asia – Peter Braidis 978-1-78952-099-6
Badfinger – Robert Day-Webb 978-1-878952-176-4
Barclay James Harvest – Keith and Monica Domone 978-1-78952-067-5
The Beatles – Andrew Wild 978-1-78952-009-5
The Beatles Solo 1969-1980 – Andrew Wild 978-1-78952-030-9
Blue Oyster Cult – Jacob Holm-Lupo 978-1-78952-007-1
Blur – Matt Bishop – 978-178952-164-1
Marc Bolan and T.Rex – Peter Gallagher 978-1-78952-124-5
Kate Bush – Bill Thomas 978-1-78952-097-2
Camel – Hamish Kuzminski 978-1-78952-040-8
Caravan – Andy Boot 978-1-78952-127-6
Cardiacs – Eric Benac 978-1-78952-131-3
Eric Clapton Solo – Andrew Wild 978-1-78952-141-2
The Clash – Nick Assirati 978-1-78952-077-4
Crosby, Stills and Nash – Andrew Wild 978-1-78952-039-2
The Damned – Morgan Brown 978-1-78952-136-8
Deep Purple and Rainbow 1968-79 – Steve Pilkington 978-1-78952-002-6
Dire Straits – Andrew Wild 978-1-78952-044-6
The Doors – Tony Thompson 978-1-78952-137-5
Dream Theater – Jordan Blum 978-1-78952-050-7
Electric Light Orchestra – Barry Delve 978-1-78952-152-8
Elvis Costello and The Attractions – Georg Purvis 978-1-78952-129-0
Emerson Lake and Palmer – Mike Goode 978-1-78952-000-2
Fairport Convention – Kevan Furbank 978-1-78952-051-4
Peter Gabriel – Graeme Scarfe 978-1-78952-138-2
Genesis – Stuart MacFarlane 978-1-78952-005-7
Gentle Giant – Gary Steel 978-1-78952-058-3
Gong – Kevan Furbank 978-1-78952-082-8
Hall and Oates – Ian Abrahams 978-1-78952-167-2
Hawkwind – Duncan Harris 978-1-78952-052-1
Peter Hammill – Richard Rees Jones 978-1-78952-163-4
Roy Harper – Opher Goodwin 978-1-78952-130-6
Jimi Hendrix – Emma Stott 978-1-78952-175-7
The Hollies – Andrew Darlington 978-1-78952-159-7
Iron Maiden – Steve Pilkington 978-1-78952-061-3
Jefferson Airplane – Richard Butterworth 978-1-78952-143-6
Jethro Tull – Jordan Blum 978-1-78952-016-3
Elton John in the 1970s – Peter Kearns 978-1-78952-034-7
The Incredible String Band – Tim Moon 978-1-78952-107-8
Iron Maiden – Steve Pilkington 978-1-78952-061-3
Judas Priest – John Tucker 978-1-78952-018-7

Kansas – Kevin Cummings 978-1-78952-057-6
The Kinks – Martin Hutchinson 978-1-78952-172-6
Korn – Matt Karpe 978-1-78952-153-5
Led Zeppelin – Steve Pilkington 978-1-78952-151-1
Level 42 – Matt Philips 978-1-78952-102-3
Little Feat – 978-1-78952-168-9
Aimee Mann – Jez Rowden 978-1-78952-036-1
Joni Mitchell – Peter Kearns 978-1-78952-081-1
The Moody Blues – Geoffrey Feakes 978-1-78952-042-2
Motorhead – Duncan Harris 978-1-78952-173-3
Mike Oldfield – Ryan Yard 978-1-78952-060-6
Opeth – Jordan Blum 978-1-78-952-166-5
Tom Petty – Richard James 978-1-78952-128-3
Porcupine Tree – Nick Holmes 978-1-78952-144-3
Queen – Andrew Wild 978-1-78952-003-3
Radiohead – William Allen 978-1-78952-149-8
Renaissance – David Detmer 978-1-78952-062-0
The Rolling Stones 1963-80 – Steve Pilkington 978-1-78952-017-0
The Smiths and Morrissey – Tommy Gunnarsson 978-1-78952-140-5
Status Quo the Frantic Four Years – Richard James 978-1-78952-160-3
Steely Dan – Jez Rowden 978-1-78952-043-9
Steve Hackett – Geoffrey Feakes 978-1-78952-098-9
Thin Lizzy – Graeme Stroud 978-1-78952-064-4
Toto – Jacob Holm-Lupo 978-1-78952-019-4
U2 – Eoghan Lyng 978-1-78952-078-1
UFO – Richard James 978-1-78952-073-6
The Who – Geoffrey Feakes 978-1-78952-076-7
Roy Wood and the Move – James R Turner 978-1-78952-008-8
Van Der Graaf Generator – Dan Coffey 978-1-78952-031-6
Yes – Stephen Lambe 978-1-78952-001-9
Frank Zappa 1966 to 1979 – Eric Benac 978-1-78952-033-0
Warren Zevon – Peter Gallagher 978-1-78952-170-2
10CC – Peter Kearns 978-1-78952-054-5

Decades Series

The Bee Gees in the 1960s – Andrew Mon Hughes et al 978-1-78952-148-1
The Bee Gees in the 1970s – Andrew Mon Hughes et al 978-1-78952-179-5
Black Sabbath in the 1970s – Chris Sutton 978-1-78952-171-9
Britpop – Peter Richard Adams and Matt Pooler 978-1-78952-169-6
Alice Cooper in the 1970s – Chris Sutton 978-1-78952-104-7
Curved Air in the 1970s – Laura Shenton 978-1-78952-069-9
Bob Dylan in the 1980s – Don Klees 978-1-78952-157-3
Fleetwood Mac in the 1970s – Andrew Wild 978-1-78952-105-4
Focus in the 1970s – Stephen Lambe 978-1-78952-079-8
Free and Bad Company in the 1970s – John Van der Kiste 978-1-78952-178-8

Genesis in the 1970s – Bill Thomas 978178952-146-7
George Harrison in the 1970s – Eoghan Lyng 978-1-78952-174-0
Marillion in the 1980s – Nathaniel Webb 978-1-78952-065-1
Mott the Hoople and Ian Hunter in the 1970s – John Van der Kiste
978-1-78-952-162-7
Pink Floyd In The 1970s – Georg Purvis 978-1-78952-072-9
Tangerine Dream in the 1970s – Stephen Palmer 978-1-78952-161-0
The Sweet in the 1970s – Darren Johnson from Gary Cosby collection 978-1-
78952-139-9
Uriah Heep in the 1970s – Steve Pilkington 978-1-78952-103-0
Yes in the 1980s – Stephen Lambe with David Watkinson 978-1-78952-125-2

On Screen series
Carry On... – Stephen Lambe 978-1-78952-004-0
David Cronenberg Patrick Chapman 978-1-78952-071-2
Doctor Who: The David Tennant Years – Jamie Hailstone 978-1-78952-066-8
James Bond – Andrew Wild – 978-1-78952-010-1
Monty Python – Steve Pilkington 978-1-78952-047-7
Seinfeld Seasons 1 to 5 – Stephen Lambe 978-1-78952-012-5

Other Books
1967: A Year In Psychedelic Rock – Kevan Furbank 978-1-78952-155-9
1970: A Year In Rock – John Van der Kiste 978-1-78952-147-4
1973: The Golden Year of Progressive Rock 978-1-78952-165-8
Babysitting A Band On The Rocks – G.D. Praetorius 978-1-78952-106-1
Eric Clapton Sessions – Andrew Wild 978-1-78952-177-1
Derek Taylor: For Your Radioactive Children – Andrew Darlington
978-1-78952-038-5
The Golden Road: The Recording History of The Grateful Dead – John Kilbride
978-1-78952-156-6
Iggy and The Stooges On Stage 1967-1974 – Per Nilsen 978-1-78952-101-6
Jon Anderson and the Warriors – the road to Yes – David Watkinson
978-1-78952-059-0
Nu Metal: A Definitive Guide – Matt Karpe 978-1-78952-063-7
Tommy Bolin: In and Out of Deep Purple – Laura Shenton 978-1-78952-070-5
Maximum Darkness – Deke Leonard 978-1-78952-048-4
Maybe I Should've Stayed In Bed – Deke Leonard 978-1-78952-053-8
The Twang Dynasty – Deke Leonard 978-1-78952-049-1

and many more to come!

Would you like to write for Sonicbond Publishing?
We are mainly a music publisher, but we also occasionally
publish in other genres including film and television. At Sonicbond
Publishing we are always on the look-out for authors, particularly for
our two main series, On Track and Decades.

Mixing fact with in depth analysis, the On Track series examines
the entire recorded work of a particular musical artist or group. All
genres are considered from easy listening and jazz to 60s soul to 90s
pop, via rock and metal.

The Decades series singles out a particular decade in an artist or
group's history and focuses on that decade in more detail than may
be allowed in the On Track series.

While professional writing experience would, of course, be
an advantage, the most important qualification is to have real
enthusiasm and knowledge of your subject. First-time authors are
welcomed, but the ability to write well in English is essential.

Sonicbond Publishing has distribution throughout Europe and
North America, and all our books are also published in E-book form.
Authors will be paid a royalty based on sales of their book.
Further details about our books are available from
www.sonicbondpublishing.com. To contact us, complete the
contact form there or email info@sonicbondpublishing.co.uk